Quote Unquote

Quote Unquote

Collected Sayings for Wise and Witty Men

Compiled by

E. W. A. CANNON

BOOKCRAFT, INC.
SALT LAKE CITY, UTAH

Library of Congress Catalog Card Number: 92-75252
ISBN 0-88494-867-6

First Printing, 1993

Printed in the United States of America

CONTENTS

Here you'll find thinking on duty and comfort
from Deity. Finding God is a more important
way to spend one's time than finding Waldo,
one has said. Relationships may be a tougher
life test than crossing the plains, observed
another.

This section is about male and female. Love
wears a mask at any age, observed one. God's
in his heaven, all right, mourned another, but
what are women doing in the marketplace
instead of home waiting for our return?

The bottom line in all living, thinking men
largely agree, is the family. But what a refreshing
viewpoint they have on the subject! Practice
of what is preached here may or may not be
reality in every bottom-line situation!

This section holds some hints for relationships—
the lighter touch with each other. Accepting each
other, as a starter, for proof of personal belief in
the ultimate fatherhood of God and in the family
of man.

A man's field of dreams stirs up the intriguing
analogy of a man's mind being like a fallow field
in spring—it waits for whatever will be planted.

Overtime is what many men say today's world is
all about. Overtime, overworked, overweight,
overburdened, over the hill. Gandhi said life is
more than picking up speed. Others insist some
people flock to the fast lane thinking they'll find
the full life. Some are overzealous. Some seek
comfort zones instead of adventures in new
responsibilities.

Empowered, to the committed Latter-day Saint
man, means "the gift that is in thee" by the "laying
on of the hands," and it's a gift that should not be
neglected (see 1 Timothy 4:14). Added one
observer, you can't build a reputation on what
you are *going* to do. And we add, the face a
man has at forty is exactly what he deserves.

RED INK 89

"Red Ink" is about sin. It's about operating in
the debit zone, the ditch, the dangerous channel—
the area of self-destruct. It's about the handwriting
on the wall and ways to get your act together.

HIGH YIELD 95

In this section Hugh B. Brown sets the tone
with the idea that a man who wants to progress
doesn't compete with others, he's interested in
surpassing himself. This section is about self-
control, the work ethic, the law of the harvest.

THINK TANK 105

Most men admit they've heard it before in every
generation for a lot of years, but "as a man thinketh"
remains the big secret to personal satisfaction about
performance. "Think Tank" tells all, including a
reminder about not being like the centipede who
overreacted to her possibilities.

I. O. U. 115

I. O. U. is another way of saying that the borrower
is in his own debt—whether he borrows money,
things, or ideas.

CHALK MARK 125

Character is made by what you stand for and
reputation by what you fall for, says one man in
"Chalk Mark." Here are fascinating perspectives

from men on how they sort out their options and
make their choices and check their checkpoints
and chalk marks.

Pocket change, the annoying but necessary loot
you drop on your nightstand before you drop
your trousers—pocket change is what is left over.
Potpourri of ideas, such as America's national
flower being the concrete cloverleaf, and if a
book is worth reading it is worth buying, and
other such pennies for thought.

Think not of football when you read "End Zone."
We are reminded in this section that life and death
are more than a game. Such mental jogs included
in this section are that when you lay down your
life you find it, and that the tragedy in life is to
end it before we've figured out how to begin it.

PREFACE

Between these covers you'll find wisdom, truth, humor, heartbreak, love notes, social lines, professional jargon, political perspective, paradigms, prophecies, and pronouncements. Great ideas come from thinking men of the past; from boys who look to a certain kind of future; from flourishing leaders and intelligentsia as well as from the elitists and the obscure among us today.

Here is diversion, direction—help in the form of perspective. There are viewpoints on a wide variety of topics. David Grayson opined that most of us have collections of sayings we live by. He said, "Whenever words fly up at me from the printed page as I read, I intercept them instantly, knowing they are for me. I turn them over carefully in my mind and cling to them hard."

Many men speak of trivia—golf scores, game results, hunting trips, money markets—but real men speak of life's challenges and possibilities. Unless we can do the latter, we'll forever be caught in the shallows instead of the mainstream.

What a man says—or what someone says he says—reveals not only his view but also maybe even his own soul. Black and white and read all over—these quotes come from the read-between-the-lines bylined columns in newsprint and the latest word in slick magazine stock, from scripture tissue, pulp stuff, vellum card, fax, and press-ready copy. Such truth has been heard as well as read here, there, and everywhere and gleaned from talk shows, boardrooms, meet-and-eat halls, sports palaces, conferences, symposia, seminars, consultations, court evidence, interviews, newscasts, theater. Heard, as well, during preachments in the sacred shrines of faith and the family circle.

Zeitgeist!

Maybe what a man says is laughed at, questioned, refuted, qualified, scoffed over, accepted as truth, copyrighted, cleared, censored, edited, or unabridged. Whatever! Paraphrased or enhanced, taken out of context even—but passed on. Quote. Unquote. What men say has been collected, clipped, and copied to share.

And now, selected and compiled here for your consideration and delight, these quotes may likely be a resource for your next up-front assignment.

The collection is separated into fourteen blocks of thought. You may begin where you have a need or scan at random. It is very good stuff. Black and white and read all over—a collection of sayings by wise and witty men.

What many men say is as good as it gets.

What God says is gospel and it lasts.

Some of each is included in *Quote Unquote.*

I acknowledge the vast heritage of thought given from one man to another and from God to man. This is a heritage of words, ideas, information, inspiration housed in the libraries of the English-speaking world. Our debt is great. Sources also include a broad dip into anthologies, collections, published and private diaries, biographies and memoirs, professional journals, holy books and histories, speeches, tombstone epitaphs, best-sellers, obscure texts—the gamut of publications and institutional periodicals. We recognize the treasure in Mother's scrapbook and Father's clipping collection. Also my own lifelong collecting.

No one is an island in the preparation of the manuscript, either. I admit the fine help from D. J. Cannon, Carla Cannon, Carrie Henderson, and the abiding, hovering editorial staff of Bookcraft.

IN GOD WE TRUST

How gentle God's commands!
How kind his precepts are!
Come, cast your burdens on the Lord
And trust his constant care.

—Philip Doddridge

Believe in God; believe that he is, and that he created all things, both in heaven and in earth; believe that he has all wisdom, and all power, both in heaven and in earth; believe that man doth not comprehend all the things which the Lord can comprehend.

—King Benjamin

I prayed about it [learning German on a mission], I worked on it, I tracted, I studied and it came to me through my efforts. You can't expect the Lord to do it all.

—Joseph Anderson

Without the assistance of that Divine Being . . . I cannot succeed. With that assistance I cannot fail.

—Abraham Lincoln

One incident where I did not obey the spirit of the Lord . . .
came pretty near costing me my life. . . .

   . . . Every man should get the Spirit of God, and then follow
its dictates. This is revelation. It doesn't make any difference
what the spirit tells you to do; it will never tell you to do
anything that is wrong.

—Wilford Woodruff

To build a house straight and strong, you do not choose crooked
boards. So to build your eternal destiny, you cannot—you must
not—limit lessons only to those warped to exclude revelation
from God.

—Russell M. Nelson

We are, on the whole, an idolatrous people—a condition most
repugnant to the Lord.

   We are . . . easily distracted from our assignment of
preparing for the coming of the Lord. . . . When threatened, we
become antienemy instead of prokingdom of God. . . .

   We forget that if we are righteous the Lord will either not
suffer our enemies to come upon us . . . or he will fight our
battles for us.

—Spencer W. Kimball

Let never day nor night unhallow'd pass,
But still remember what the Lord hath done.

—William Shakespeare

Four score and seven years ago our fathers brought forth on this continent, a new nation, conceived in Liberty, and dedicated to the proposition that all men are created equal.

Now we are engaged in a great civil war, testing whether that nation, or any nation so conceived and so dedicated, can long endure. We are met on a great battle-field of that war. We have come to dedicate a portion of that field, as a final resting place for those who here gave their lives that that nation might live. It is altogether fitting and proper that we should do this.

But, in a larger sense, we can not dedicate—we can not consecrate—we can not hallow—this ground. The brave men, living and dead, who struggled here, have consecrated it, far above our poor power to add or detract. The world will little note, nor long remember what we say here, but it can never forget what they did here. It is for us the living, rather, to be dedicated here to the unfinished work which they who fought here have thus far so nobly advanced. It is rather for us to be here dedicated to the great task remaining before us—that from these honored dead we take increased devotion to that cause for which they gave the last full measure of devotion—that we here highly resolve that these dead shall not have died in vain—that this nation, under God, shall have a new birth of freedom—and that government of the people, by the people, for the people, shall not perish from the earth.

—Abraham Lincoln

The message of this general conference [October 1992] of The Church of Jesus Christ of Latter-day Saints is that there is but one guiding hand in the universe, only one truly infallible light, one unfailing beacon to the world. That light is Jesus Christ.

—Howard W. Hunter

I went to the [University of Utah] from 1951 to 1957. . . . The faculty at the Salt Lake Institute during that time—Lowell L. Bennion, T. Edgar Lyon, and George Boyd, as well as Elder Marion D. Hanks . . . —were all brilliant thinkers and teachers and also devoted Latter-day Saints. And because they were deeply involved, and were *known* by their students and others to be deeply involved, in serving the poor and deprived throughout the Salt Lake Valley, they spoke with the unique authority of practicing Christians.

. . . When they told us the Church was true despite our human failings, we trusted them.

—Eugene England

M*yth: I don't have to repent right now. I can do whatever I want until I'm ready to go on my mission (or get married in the temple) and then repent.*

There's a certain devilish logic to this point. But while it's true that young people may repent of sin and may still enjoy the blessings of missionary service and temple marriage, many others are denied those privileges because they are unable to escape patterns of disobedience established during their teen years.

—Joseph Walker

For behold, I, God, have suffered these things for all, that they might not suffer if they would repent; but if they would not repent they must suffer even as I.

—Jesus Christ

Lord God of Hosts, be with us yet,
Lest we forget—lest we forget!

—*Rudyard Kipling*

No one could tell me where my soul might be.
I searched for God and he eluded me.
I sought my brother out and found all three,
My brother, soul, and Thee.

—*Quoted by Robert E. Thompson*

The one great God looked down and smiled
And counted each his loving child;
For Turk, and Brahmin, Monk, and Jew
Had reached Him through the Gods they knew.

—*Harry Romaine*

I believe in Christianity like I believe the sun will rise—not
because it comes up in the morning but because I see everything
else by it.

—*C. S. Lewis*

Methods of change are ours. Principles are the Lord's.

—*Richard L. Evans*

Let's suppose . . . that a person . . . rejects the idea that there is a spiritual dimension to life. . . . Revelation [then] is rejected because the reality of God is rejected. Deciding what is good and bad, therefore, will not be dependent on any set of God-given laws or fear of eternal consequences.

—Gerald N. Lund

We are all of us by birth the offspring of God—more nearly related to Him than we are to one another; for in Him we live and move and have our being.

—William Law

The Lord works from the inside out. The world works from the outside in. The world would take people out of the slums. Christ takes the slums out of people, and then they take themselves out of the slums.

—Ezra Taft Benson

More purity give me,
More strength to o'ercome,
More freedom from earthstains,
More longing for home.
More fit for the kingdom,
More used would I be,
More blessed and holy—
More, Savior, like thee.

—Philip Paul Bliss

True peace consists in not separating ourselves from the will of God.

—*Thomas Aquinas*

If we do what's right we have no need to fear.

—*Evan Stephens*

We feel, our Father, that this assemblage needs thy Holy Spirit to be with them. They need thy help, so that in the consideration of the great and important questions that shall enter into their discussions, they may be filled with that feeling that cometh from thee . . .

—*George Q. Cannon*
(Utah constitutional meeting)

I am come that they might have life, and that they might have it more abundantly.

—*Jesus Christ*

[At the Jerusalem dead letter office I] receive one hundred sacks of mail a day addressed to the highest Deity; and since Jews, Muslims, and Christians all hold Jerusalem holy, it comes from a wide assortment of seekers. I would deliver the mail in person, but my connections are not that good!

—*Ben-Meir*

In the service of the Lord, it is not where you serve but how.

—*J. Reuben Clark, Jr.*

Let not our hearts be busy inns
That have no room for thee,
But cradles for the living Christ
And His nativity.

—*Ralph Spaulding*

Faithful prayer is never just a conversation with oneself.

—*Truman G. Madsen*

He asks of you . . . the sacrifice of your sins—the hardest thing
in the world to give up! But the promise is crystal clear, "If you
will purify yourselves, sanctify yourselves, I will bless you."
And I'm afraid the postscript is, "And if you don't, I can't."

—*Truman G. Madsen*

Give me chastity and continency, but do not give it yet.

—*Augustine*

Let any man today join issue with the sins of our times and, like Christ, he too will discover the inevitable cross.

—George E. Dawkins

[Faith] is also betting your life that in the character of Christ we are privileged to see what kind of being God is.

—Charles Clayton Morrison

The Lord seeth not as man seeth; for man looketh on the outward appearance, but the Lord looketh on the heart.

—1 Samuel 16:7

I know the Savior lives. He is there for me! He lifts me when I am down. I am glad I know this.

—Blake Allen (age eighteen)

Faith is betting your life there is a God.

—Donald Hankey

Choose you this day whom ye will serve; . . . but as for me and my house, we will serve the Lord.

—Joshua

The gospel of Christ is not an escape from the hard realities of life. . . . Both the person who follows Christ and the person who mocks Him live in the world among the same men and where the same laws of nature operate.

—Lowell L. Bennion

However cowardly or courageous we prove ourselves to be, there is no question about the courage of Christ. With uncompromising firmness He refused to submit to the dead level of His times and people. . . . It cost Him His life. Yet every courageous follower of Christ comes to know the truth of His promise: "Blessed are they which are persecuted for righteousness' sake: for theirs is the kingdom of heaven."

—Obert C. Tanner

For God regards the greatness of the love that prompts a man rather than the greatness of his achievement.

—Thomas à Kempis

I observed that as I believed in the work [of the Lord] that I received the manifestations of the spirit of God.

—Jared Carter

There have been men before now who got so interested in proving the existence of God that they came to care nothing for God Himself. . . . There have been some who were so occupied in spreading Christianity that they never gave a thought to Christ.

—C. S. Lewis

The voice of the Lord came to [the Nephites] in their afflictions, saying: Lift up your heads and be of good comfort. . . .

. . . I will also ease the burdens which are put upon your shoulders, that even you cannot feel them upon your backs, even while you are in bondage; and this will I do that ye may stand as witnesses for me hereafter, and that ye may know of a surety that I, the Lord God, do visit my people in their afflictions.

And . . . the Lord did strengthen them that they could bear up their burdens with ease, and they did submit cheerfully and with patience to all the will of the Lord.

And . . . the voice of the Lord came unto them again, saying: Be of good comfort, for on the morrow I will deliver you out of bondage.

—Mosiah 24:13–16

The first precept of the divine law, therefore, indeed its sum and substance, is to love God unconditionally as the Supreme God— unconditionally, I say, and not from any love or fear of aught besides.

—Baruch Spinoza

Be it known unto all nations, kindreds, tongues, and people, unto whom this work [the Book of Mormon] shall come: That we, through the grace of God the Father, and our Lord Jesus Christ, have seen the plates which contain this record, which is a record of the people of Nephi, and also of the Lamanites, their brethren, and also of the people of Jared, who came from the tower of which hath been spoken. And we also know that they have been translated by the gift and power of God, for his voice hath declared it unto us; wherefore we know of a surety that the work is true. And we also testify that we have seen the engravings which are upon the plates; and they have been shown unto us by the power of God, and not of man. And we declare with words of soberness, that an angel of God came down from heaven, and he brought and laid before our eyes, that we beheld and saw the plates, and the engravings thereon; and we know that it is by the grace of God the Father, and our Lord Jesus Christ, that we beheld and bear record that these things are true. And it is marvelous in our eyes. Nevertheless, the voice of the Lord commanded us that we should bear record of it; wherefore, to be obedient unto the commandments of God, we bear testimony of these things. And we know that if we are faithful in Christ, we shall rid our garments of the blood of all men, and be found spotless before the judgment-seat of Christ, and shall dwell with him eternally in the heavens. And the honor be to the Father, and to the Son, and to the Holy Ghost, which is one God. Amen.

—Oliver Cowdery
—David Whitmer
—Martin Harris

God has no need for our worship. It is we who need to show our gratitude for what we have received.

—Thomas Aquinas

No wicked man could write such a book as this [the Book of Mormon]; and no good man would write it, unless it were true and he were commanded of God to do so.

—*George Cannon*

[David Whitmer] told me in all the solemnity of his advanced years, that the testimony he had given to the world, and which was published in the Book of Mormon, was true, every word of it.

—*James N. Moyle*

And therefore will the Lord wait, that he may be gracious unto you, and therefore will he be exalted, that he may have mercy upon you: for the Lord is a God of judgment: blessed are all they that wait for him.

—*Isaiah*

Be still, and know that I am God.

—*Psalm 46:10*

I can do all things through Christ which strengtheneth me.

—*Paul*

I know that God lives. I know that Jesus lives, for I have seen Him. I know that this is the Church of God and that it is founded on Jesus Christ, our Redeemer. I testify to you of these things as one that knows—as one of the Apostles of the Lord Jesus Christ that can bear witness to you today in the presence of the Lord Jesus Christ that He lives and that He will live and will come to reign on the earth to sway an undisputed scepter.

—*George Q. Cannon*

The things of God are of deep import; and time, and experience, and careful and ponderous and solemn thoughts can only find them out. Thy mind, O man! if thou wilt lead a soul unto salvation, must stretch as high as the utmost heavens, and search into and contemplate the darkest abyss, and the broad expanse of eternity—thou must commune with God. How much more dignified and noble are the thoughts of God, than the vain imaginations of the human heart!

—*Joseph Smith*

The Lord Jesus Christ appeared to me at the time of the death of President Woodruff. He instructed me to go right ahead and reorganize the First Presidency of the Church at once and not wait as had been done after the death of the previous presidents, and that I was to succeed President Woodruff. . . . He stood right here, about three feet above the floor. . . . I want you to remember that this is the testimony of your grandfather, that he told you with his own lips that he actually saw the Savior, here in the temple, and talked with him face to face.

—*Lorenzo Snow*

Look unto God with firmness of mind, and pray unto him with exceeding faith, and he will console you in your afflictions, and he will plead your cause, and send down justice upon those who seek your destruction.

—Jacob (Nephite prophet)

There is a kind of communication that is also unmeasurable. It takes place at the level of feelings. It is just as real as that communication which *is* measurable. It is communication of the Spirit. It is the way that God most frequently communicates with each of us.

—Paul N. Clayton

Behold, are not the things that God hath wrought marvelous in our eyes? Yea, and who can comprehend the marvelous works of God?

—Moroni

I was without hope . . . ; for they repented not of their iniquities, but did struggle for their lives without calling upon that Being who created them.

—Mormon

Trust in Allah, but tie up your camel.

—Turkish proverb

God gives me strength and sustenance
When failure comes my way.
He gives me hope and courage
To face each newborn day.
He helps me in my hour of need
In answer to my prayer.

—*Harold F. Mohn*

The years I've spent at the University Medical Center as a volunteer clergyman were the most compelling and satisfying of anything I have ever done. Without exception, I have noted that when people of any faith turn to Heavenly Father for help in their time of deep crisis, he is there for them. He lifts their burdens, as he has promised! Without fail. Each week in our little sacrament meeting held for patients, their families, and staff of the hospital, I'd look out over seventy to one hundred people—people with ravaging illnesses or coping with crushing accidents—and always they'd be upbeat and full of faith. It was an incredible lesson for me. The Lord was lifting their burdens! How can people know this if they haven't been to the hospital under demanding circumstances?

—*Dilworth C. Strasser*

Try to live so that you can have the Spirit with you in all your activities. Pray for the spirit of discernment that you may hear the promptings of the Spirit and understand them. And then pray for courage to do them, to follow the guidance of the Spirit.

—*Marion G. Romney*

MERGER: MALE/FEMALE

There can be no heaven without righteous women.

—Spencer W. Kimball

Any man that marries a wife by any other authority than the authority of the Holy Priesthood is simply married for time, "or until death do you part." When you go into the Spirit world you have no claim on your wife and children. The ordinance of having them sealed to you by one having the authority of the Holy Priesthood must be attended to in this world.

—Wilford Woodruff

A happy, mutually satisfying marriage will not long survive tactics of force, regardless of the reason. A successful eternal marriage must be built slowly and carefully, on a foundation of individual agency.

—Larry K. Langlois

Dregs of love as sweet as the first sip warm our precious numbered days.

—Hugh Miller

The privileges and requirements of the gospel are fundamentally alike for men and women. . . .

This makes individuals of man and woman—individuals with the right of free agency, with the power of individual decision, with individual opportunity for everlasting joy, whose own actions throughout the eternities, with the loving aid of the Father, will determine individual achievement.

—John A. Widtsoe

Let your maidservant be faithful, strong—and homely.

—Benjamin Franklin

I have found it impossible to carry the heavy burden of responsibility and to discharge my duties as King as I would wish to do without the help and support of the woman I love.

—Edward VIII

Our marriage has been based on a combination of mutual trusting, sharing of mutual interests, and the kind of love that is thoughtful and continuing.

—Wallace F. Bennett

[An] absentee father is no comedy for the woman left behind.

—Clarence Page

Many men seem to fall off the horse on one side or the other. Some do not fully understand their roles as patriarchs in their own homes, and thus literally abdicate their leadership position. But others fail to understand that revelation for the family does not always come directly through him. . . . [His] wife in particular can be in close touch with the divine source of wisdom.

—Ed J. Pinegar

Do you know what is great about my wife? She does the dirty work, all right, and lovingly—but with gloves on!

—Robbie Dermott

Married people should never travel together. They blame one another for everything that goes wrong.

—George Bernard Shaw

I need so much the quiet of your love
    After the day's loud strife.

—Charles Hanson Towne

A place in thy memory, dearest,
    Is all that I claim. . . .

As a sister remembers a brother,
Oh, dearest, remember me.

—Gerald Griffin

The heart that has truly loved never forgets.

—Thomas Moore

An old sweetheart of mine!—Is this her presence here with me,
Or but a vain creation of a lover's memory? . . .

But, ah! my dream is broken by a step upon the stair,
And the door is softly opened, and—my wife is standing there;
Yet with eagerness and rapture all my vision I resign,—
To greet the *living* presence of that old sweetheart of mine.

—James Whitcomb Riley

Say I'm weary, say I'm sad;
    Say that health and wealth have missed me;
Say I'm growing old, but add—
        Jenny kissed me!

—Leigh Hunt

Let's contend no more, Love,
    Strive nor weep:
All be as before, Love.

—Robert Browning

I love you,
Not only for what you are,
But for what I am
When I am with you.

—Roy Croft

Oh, come with me and be my love! . . .

Oh, come if the love thou hast for me
Is pure and fresh as mine for thee.

—Major Calder Campbell

I sometimes wonder if people realize the purpose of their existence, and the importance of the labor that men and women are expected to perform while on the earth.

—George Albert Smith

The differences between women and men create conflict, but conflict used creatively can produce growth and synergy.

—Richard J. Anderson

Now I see things differently. For example, I now realize my wife's spiritual growth is also my personal [concern]. It is not that I can say, "I'm going to do this on my own. I'll help her, but if she doesn't do it, that is her problem."

What I pray for most is that the Lord will forgive our weaknesses and help us to strive to do our very best to make these promises possible in our lives. Now we have to plan our spiritual growth together as husband and wife, as a family. We shall read the scriptures together. We shall grow together.

—Joseph Sitati

The single most important strength at that time in my life was my personal relationship with my Father in Heaven and my Savior, Jesus Christ. They knew the true intent of my heart and because my marriage ended in divorce did not mean that I nor my former spouse were failures. Nor was our marriage. Many moments will be cherished forever.

Many good-meaning individuals are taken aback by a divorce of a beloved couple. Their ways of dealing with it are almost as numerous as the individuals themselves. Some back away completely. Others say things that just don't come out the way they intended, resulting in hurt feelings. But it must be remembered that each of us is striving for perfection. Words may be said or judgments made. But remember you are a child of God.

—Lynn W. Meikle

I have such sweet thoughts. I have had wealth, rank, and power; but if these were all I had, how wretched I should be!

—Prince Albert

There have always been more husbands and wives who remain true to their marriage vows than those who stray. We would be prudent to remember that Satan is the father of lies. He has no scruples. . . . It is his method to use the media to spread the illusion that marriage is an obsolete, even undesirable institution.

—Victor L. Brown, Jr.

If a wife's worries and concerns are the determinative factor for assuring the success of a talk in general conference, then I'm happy to say I've got it made, for the amount of worries and concerns generated by my wife is more than enough to assure the success of not only my talk, but also all of the talks that have been given and will be given from this pulpit at this conference. What a blessing to have a wife who worries for you and over you.

—Sam K. Shimabukuro

Music I heard with you was more than music, and bread I broke with you was more than bread.

—Conrad Aiken

I don't speak German and he doesn't speak English, but I think I just agreed to marry his daughter.

—Jeff Hammerschmidt

Advice to widowers: Look for a nurse with a purse.

—*Lyle McLean Ward*

A [leader's] spouse picks up things informally that are not meant to be brought to his official attention. . . . Spouses are a whole different level or channel . . . to pass along those things . . . meant to reach [a] husband's ear.

—*Charles Young*

Be so close to those you love that when they weep you taste salt.

—*Boris Pasternak*

Attention, women! If you're looking for a state where there won't be much competition, why not choose Wyoming? There are only 44,000 women over sixty in the entire state. Of course, the down side is there aren't that many men there, either.

—*Joe Volz*

To love means to commit oneself without guarantee, to give oneself completely in the hope that our love will parallel love in the loved person. Love is an act of faith, and whosoever is of little faith is also of little love.

—*Erich Fromm*

If it must be so, let's not weep or complain.
If I have failed, or you, or life turned sullen,
We have had these things; they do not come again.
But the flag still flies and the city has not fallen.

—Humbert Wolfe

The ability which high friendship demands is ability to do
without it. That high office requires great and sublime parts.
There must be very two before there can be very one. Let it be
an alliance of too large, formidable natures, mutually feared,
before yet they recognize the deep identity which beneath these
disparities unites them.

—Ralph Waldo Emerson

In every affair, consider what precedes and follows, and then
undertake it.

—Epictetus

Consider what comes next before you make the move, take the
step, respond to an urge.

—D. J. Cannon

Hell is truth seen too late.

—Sterling W. Sill

Love is to the moral nature what the sun is to the earth.

—*Honoré de Balzac*

They [women] are wiser than men because they know less and understand more.

—*James Stephens*

A word too much, or a kiss too long,
And the world is never the same again.

—*Author unknown*

Not in my car you won't.

—*Stanford P. Darger*

There are women who have changed the face of the world as we know it, enriched the intellectual content of our lives, and are— not to put too fine a point on it—aesthetically appealing. There is, of course, no wrong time to love or honor women, and we do so every day. This year, however, has been particularly rewarding. In politics, considering how well men have proven they can run things, we will undoubtedly send a few more women to Washington!

—*Terry McDonnell*

A life without love in it is like a heap of ashes upon a deserted hearth with the fire dead, the laughter stilled, the light extinguished.

—Frank P. Tebbetts

I am the poet of the woman
    the same as the man,
And I say it is as great to be
    a woman as to be a man,
And I say there is nothing
    greater than the mother of men.

—Walt Whitman

Never strike your wife, even with a flower.

—Hindu proverb

Brethren, we need to reaffirm our resolve to be more helpful in the home. We heard about one of your wives who was awakened by the clanging of the garbage collectors. With her hair in rollers and her face shiny with rejuvenating cream, she sleepily leaned out the window and called to the collectors, "Am I too late for the garbage?"

"Certainly not," replied the garbage collector. "Hop right in."

—Keith Engar

Johnny: Phyllis, I am so sorry you and Fang are getting a
    divorce.
Phyllis: Yes . . . well, it couldn't be helped. He brought a book
    to bed every night.
Johnny: But Phyllis, a lot of people like to read in bed.
Phyllis: Yes . . . well, his reading is one thing, but it was
    coloring those pictures that got to me.

Friend: Where's Joe?
Joe's Wife: Home.
Friend: Why didn't he come?
Joe's Wife: He said at last he's old enough now that he doesn't
    have to do anything he doesn't want to do anymore.
Friend: Yeah?
Joe's Wife: Yeah! And he said he didn't want to come.

—*Lowell Gary Anderson*

There is an answer to the passionate longings of the heart . . .
that is to live outside yourself in love.

—*Robert Browning*

BOTTOM LINE

The bottom line of life is that families are supposed to want to be together forever—here and hereafter, you see.

—John Ajax

Advice for a teenage daughter, five inexpensive beauty hints:
For attractive lips, speak words of kindness;
For lovely eyes, seek out the good in people;
For a slim figure, share your food with the hungry;
For beautiful hair, let a child run his fingers through it once a
    day;
And, for poise, walk with the knowledge that you will never
    walk alone.

—Sam Levenson

Have nothing in your houses that you do not know to be useful, or believe to be beautiful.

—William Morris

A boy can make a baby. It takes a dad to raise one.

—Jesse Jackson

There is no substitute for the home. Its foundation is as ancient as the world, and its mission has been ordained of God from the earliest times.

—Joseph F. Smith

As we speak of the great men in history, we frequently refer to their home life, with a fireside about which the family met, a saintly mother, a period of devotion, the reading of the Sacred Word, a family prayer. Out of such an atmosphere our great men acquired an attitude of self-reliance, an enterprising spirit, a willingness to work, with honesty and integrity as guiding stars, and a due regard for the teachings of the Almighty.

Is each American family today contributing in this manner to our national greatness?

—Mark E. Petersen

One father is worth more than a hundred school masters.

—George Herbert

When the upper and lower ranks in society have a family feeling for each other, this means human happiness.

—Lichi Ching Chieh

If you could give your child the key to open a window to the world, would you do it? If you could strengthen your relationship with your child, become a partner in adventure and enchantment, help your child feel compassion, courage, and tolerance for others, wouldn't you do it? What if you could do all these things in only fifteen minutes a day?

You can. All you have to do is read to your child.

—*Thomas R. Lee*

When a child has been baptized and confirmed a member of this Church, and the hands of authorized servants of God are placed upon his or her head, and is promised the gift of the Holy Ghost, because of clean minds and bodies, they will and do receive the Holy Ghost. . . .

You cannot tell me that children cannot bear their testimonies under the inspiration and divine direction of the Holy Ghost.

—*Joseph L. Wirthlin*

Consider every area in your home as a site for clutter—If you are not using an item *now,* get rid of it. Expecting something to come in handy "sometime" . . . is no reason to keep things.

—*Jeff Campbell*

What I like more than anything is to go to schools and talk to kids. [I tell them] a friend will not discourage you if you want to play piano or dance or sing. A friend will not offer you drugs.

—Gregory Hines

In our family, there was no clear line between religion and fly fishing.

—Norman Maclean

—Homes are not democracies.
—Good parents discipline before the stares of others tell them to.
—Children have no inalienable right to filibuster.
—Our children's TVs should not be bigger and better than ours.

—Fred Grossman

In order to bring down the blessings of heaven, we must be actively making peace in the home, the office, the social groups we move in, the Church, the classroom, the neighborhood, the community, the world.

—Robert E. Wells

When the telemarketer calls and asks to speak to the head of the household, many honest parents would have to hand the phone to their children.

—Fred Grossman

Parents, teachers, and leaders who strive to live and teach gospel principles can be assured that they will not be held accountable for the sins of those over whom they have been given charge, for symbolically, their own "garments" are spotless.

—Keith H. Meservy

Many of us have the perception that we are a very mobile society. Despite this, we still have a population that lives in close proximity to their immediate families.

—Peter A. Rogerson

When elected officials quit listening to their constituency, people have no choice but to express outrage. The Park City Board of Education seems to have forgotten that we have a representative form of government.

To state that "parents practically run the place" is something to be proud of, not something of which to be ashamed.

—Steve L. Haugen

Thank your mother for the nice dinner—then you may be excused.

—Sylvester Q. Cannon

When anyone asks me how many grandchildren we have—and in our town everyone is always asking—I have a ready answer: Who knows?

—Frank Santiago

A late nineteenth-century ideal of [our] fledgling magazine [was that] a beautiful house furthered the good life, both morally and aesthetically. . . . We continue to ponder and define that noble concept, the house beautiful.

—Louis Oliver Grapp

1. Never swing at the first pitch.
2. Because I said so.
3. There's no "i" in team.
4. Don't do anything you'll be ashamed to tell me in the morning.

—Robert Masillo

Babies do not want to hear about babies; they like to be told of giants and castles and of something which can stretch their little minds.

—Samuel Johnson

I want my children to show proper respect to all men and be gentle to them, as you wish they would be gentle to you. Be subject to all the officers, both civil and religious, and reverence them in their offices. When you speak of the Prophet and the Apostles, speak well of them and not reproachfully.

—Heber C. Kimball

A lady was asked if she had children, and she replied that she had two. The host then asked, "And what are they?" And the woman replied, "They're both Protestants."

—John Pepper (Belfast journalist)

Human beings are the only creatures on earth that allow their children to come back home.

—Bill Cosby

Attempting to force others to accept our way of thinking will cause them to close their minds to our teachings and ultimately reject our words. They have their free agency.

—Dallas N. Archibald

The battle to feed all humanity is over. In the 1970s the world will undergo famines—*hundreds* of millions of people will starve to death.

—Paul Ehrlich

I would like to know what you have done with my name.

—George A. Smith (to grandson George Albert Smith)

Let no man despise thy youth; but be thou an example of the believers, in word, in conversation, in charity, in spirit, in faith, in purity.

—Paul

O remember, remember, my son, . . . how strict are the commandments of God. And he said: If ye will keep my commandments ye shall prosper in the land—but if ye keep not his commandments ye shall be cut off from his presence.

—Alma

While the Church's welfare system provides temporarily for those it helps, it also focuses on strengthening the family, teaching a vigorous work ethic, and helping the needy to help themselves. The Mormon culture encourages the belief that welfare is a last resort.

—Tucker Carlson

Parents know a lot more about what is going on and why than most of us think. . . . I think parents, along with teenagers, grow up a lot quicker now!

—Jensen Harris

Coed slumber parties for teenagers? You've got to be kidding. Parents are getting dumber every year.

—*Richard Metcalf*

And he shall turn the heart of the fathers to the children, and the heart of the children to their fathers.

—*Malachi 4:6*

It doesn't matter where a boy comes from as long as he knows where he is going.

—*John Warnick*

SOFTWARE

We need more of the light touch. . . . God tells us to be peaceful. . . . How much more a person can accomplish if he will adopt a peaceable attitude rather than one of aggression. He does not have to be soft or weak; he can perform his duty with evident kindness and goodwill.

—D. J. Cannon

[Ask] not what my quorum can do for me, but what I can do for my quorum.

—S. Dilworth Young

I believe in people. I love, need, and respect people above all else, including the arts, natural scenery, organized piety, or nationalistic superstructures. One human figure on the slope of a mountain can make the whole mountain disappear for me. One person fighting for the truth can disqualify for me the platitudes of centuries. And one human being who meets with injustice can render invalid the entire system which had dispensed it.

—Leonard Bernstein

Powerful insights have drawn me gently but firmly closer to the principle of mercy, a core doctrine some of us miss.

—Douglas D. Alder

He was a friend to man, and lived in a house by the side of the road.

—Homer

Not understood. How many breasts are aching,
    For lack of sympathy? Ah! day to day,
How many cheerless, lonely hearts are breaking!
    How many noble spirits pass away,
        Not understood.

—Thomas Bracken

Make new friends, but keep the old.
Those are silver, these are gold.

—Joseph Parry

And things can never go badly wrong
If the heart to be true and the love be strong.

—George Macdonald

He drew a circle that shut me out—
Heretic, rebel, a thing to flout.
But Love and I had the wit to win:
We drew a circle that took him in!

—Edwin Markham

Always remember there are two types of people in this world: those who come into a room and say, "Well, here I am!" and those who come in and say, "Ah, there you are!"

—*Frederick L. Collins*

If we are to repair our democratic institutions, the first thing we must do is to learn to talk to one another again.

—*William Greider*

Sam Walton understood people the way Thomas Edison understood innovation and Henry Ford understood production. He gave something of value to everyone he touched.

—*Jack Welch*

Amiability and good temper do not come easily when one is hungry.

—*A. J. Cronin*

I wanted to evoke the joys of childhood and being in love when I created the title number from *Singin' in the Rain*. . . . I wanted to bring audiences back to their childhoods when they would cavort in the rain, even though their mothers would give them trouble. . . . I also wanted to make them feel like they were in love. A fellow in love does silly things.

—*Gene Kelly*

For the withholding of love is the negation of the spirit of Christ, the proof that we never knew Him, that for us He lived in vain. It means that He suggested nothing in all our thoughts, that He inspired nothing in all our lives, that we were not once near enough to Him to be seized with the spell of His compassion for the world. It means that:

> "I lived for myself, I thought for myself,
> For myself, and none beside—
> Just as if Jesus had never lived,
> As if He had never died."

—Henry Drummond

Those who bring sunshine to the life of others cannot keep it from themselves.

—J. M. Barrie

I want to believe that even Hitler is my brother, that we once lived in love and peace and that through the power of mercy we can do so again. I want to believe that the very worst is redeemable—because then I am too. Surely that is the most remarkable quality of mercy.

—Eugene England

A Christian . . . believes in plain and simple living and high thinking.

—Lowell L. Bennion

What doth the Lord require of thee, but to do justly, and to love mercy, and to walk humbly with thy God?

—Micah

So still it must be said "the judgments of the Lord, are true and righteous altogether."

With malice toward none; with charity for all; with firmness in the right, as God gives us to see the right, let us strive on to finish the work we are in.

—Abraham Lincoln

If you want action, let people know what is expected of them. For example, there is the story of the museum guide who was just finishing the tour, saying, "And here, ladies and gentlemen, at the close, this splendid Greek statue. Note the noble way in which the neck supports the head, the splendid curve of the shoulders, and, ladies and gentlemen, note the natural way in which the open hand is stretched out, as if to emphasize, 'Don't forget a tip for the guide.'"

—Maxwell Droke

Enquire not what boils in another's pot.

—Thomas Fuller

We then that are strong ought to bear the infirmities of the weak, and not to please ourselves.

—Paul

There is a destiny that makes us brothers;
   None goes his way alone:
All that we send into the lives of others
   Comes back into our own.

—Edwin Markham

We must love brotherly without dissimulation; we must love
one another with a pure heart fervently. We must bear one
another's burthens. We must not look only on our own things,
but also on the things of our brethren. . . .

   . . . We must . . . rejoice together, mourn together, labour and
suffer together.

—John Winthrop

Teach me to love and to forgive,
Exact my own defects to scan,
What others are, to feel,
And know myself a Man.

—Thomas Gray

The moment of friendship—we cannot tell the precise moment
when a friendship is formed. As in filling a vessel drop by drop
there is at last a drop which makes it run over, so in a series of
kindnesses there is at last one that makes the heart run over.

—Samuel Johnson

The gospel teaches diligence and honesty and conscientiousness. And even more important, the gospel teaches us to be kind. . . . When I go out of my way to help someone, people are often surprised. But they sense that I am sincere, that I really care.

—Joo Duck Young

For it is in giving that we receive;
It is in pardoning that we are pardoned; and
It is in dying that we are born to eternal life.

—Francis of Assisi

They [Amazonian tribal leaders] . . . tied this woven strand around my wrist with a special knot, a symbol of their trust. They told me their prophets had forecast a day when the white people would be in trouble and would need their knowledge to save the earth.

—Maurice Strong

There seems to be a basic drive for independence in all of us, from the first "I'll do it myself" of a toddler to the "I don't want to be a burden to anyone" of an older person. This is one reason care giving and the feelings it arouses are unsettling.

The recipient of care often wants no more than a sense of dignity and purpose. The care givers, wrestling with the constraints of time and money, are themselves constantly reminded that they, too, may need care someday.

—Horace B. Deets

A real friend is one who walks in when the rest of the world walks out.

—Walter Winchell

He is my friend," I said—
"Be patient!" Overhead
The skies were dreary and dim
And lo! the thought of him
Smiled on my heart and then
The sun shone out again!

—James Whitcomb Riley

Ointment and perfume rejoice the heart: so doth the sweetness of a man's friend by hearty counsel.

—Proverbs 27:9

I give not because I have not, but if I had I would give.

—King Benjamin

Sam's role was basically one of supporting and assisting his more acclaimed younger brother, and he ultimately received all the blessings promised to Nephi and his posterity.

—Howard W. Hunter

Degeneration flourished because of the wickedness of the king [Noah] and the priests. . . . It was because of the bad example of the leaders that the people fell into wrongdoing. Pointing out this cause-and-effect relationship is a major contribution of the story. People have a tendency to follow their leaders, and corrupt leaders corrupt the whole kingdom.

—Robert J. Matthews

If we could read the secret history of our enemies, we should find in each man's life sorrow and suffering enough to disarm all hostility.

—Henry Wadsworth Longfellow

What sweetness is left in life, if you take away friendship? Robbing life of friendship is like robbing the world of the sun.

—Cicero

The only way to have a friend is to be one.

—Ralph Waldo Emerson

Service life is not freedom. It can be a contented slavery, though.

—T. E. Lawrence

Love is something eternal—the aspect may change, but not the essence. There is the same difference in a person before and after he is in love as there is in an unlighted lamp and one that is burning. The lamp was there and it was a good lamp, but now it is shedding light, too, and that is its real function.

—Vincent van Gogh

Blessed is the man who can enjoy the small things, the common beauties, the little day-by-day events; sunshine on the fields, . . . a friend passing by. So many people who go afield for enjoyment leave it behind them at home.

—David Grayson

To have friends whose lives we can elevate or depress by our influence is sacred. To be entrusted with little children is sacred. To have powers by which we can make this earth a more decent place is sacred. . . . For when anyone vitally believes that anything is sacred, he will shrink from sacrilege.

—Harry Emerson Fosdick

May the peace of our Father in Heaven abide in your hearts and in the hearts of people everywhere as they draw near to Him in prayer and in praise this Christmastide. And may the sick be restored; may the sorrowing be comforted; may the lonely have their hearts lifted; and the weary be rested; the needy be fed; may the doubting receive assurance and may evil and designing men be confounded.

—David O. McKay

I would be a friend to the friendless and find joy in ministering to the needs of the poor.

I would visit the sick and afflicted and inspire in them a desire for faith to be healed.

I would teach the truth to the understanding and blessing of all mankind.

I would seek out the erring one and try to win him back to a righteous and a happy life.

I would not seek to force people to live up to my ideals but rather love them into doing the thing that is right.

I would live with the masses and help to solve their problems that their earth life may be happy.

I would avoid the publicity of high positions and discourage the flattery of thoughtless friends.

I would not knowingly wound the feelings of any, not even one who may have wronged me, but would seek to do him good and make him my friend.

I would overcome the tendency to selfishness and jealousy and rejoice in the successes of all the children of my Heavenly Father.

I would not be an enemy to any living soul.

Knowing that the Redeemer of mankind has offered to the world the only plan that will fully develop us and make us really happy here and hereafter, I feel it not only a duty but also a blessed privilege to disseminate this truth.

—George Albert Smith

If one by one we counted people out
For the least sin, it wouldn't take us long
To get so we had no one left to live with.
For to be social is to be forgiving.

—Robert Frost

To be capable of steady friendship and lasting love is the proof, not only of goodness of heart, but of strength of mind.

—*William Hazlitt*

Will you be my friend?
    For no reason that I know
    Except I want you so.

—*James Kanaugh*

Put yourself in harmony with the things among which your lot is cast; love those with whom you have your portion with a true love.

—*Marcus Aurelius*

Always remember that the human heart is tender, and each individual is precious to our Heavenly Father.

—*David O. McKay*

There are two virtues, two ethical principles, that embrace all the virtues of life. They are integrity and love. . . . Love presupposes integrity, and integrity needs the direction love can give it.

—*Lowell L. Bennion*

To me, you are still nothing more than a boy who is just like a hundred thousand other little boys. And I have no need of you. And you, on your part, have no need of me. To you, I am nothing more than a fox like a hundred thousand other foxes. But if you tame me, then we shall need each other. To me, you will be unique in all the world. To you, I shall be unique in all the world. . . .

If you tame me, it will be as if the sun came to shine on my life. I shall know the sound of a step that will be different from all the others.

—*Antoine de Saint-Exupéry*

If you forgive people enough, you belong to them, and they to you, whether either person likes it or not—squatter's rights of the heart.

—*John Hilton*

It has indeed been said that Lawrence of Arabia would have survived (as would Edward FitzGerald without *Omar Khayyám*) if only as a letter writer.

—*Ronald Storrs*

Slowly starved, still [the Russian scientists during war] refused to eat from any of their collection containers of rice, peas, corn, and wheat. And posterity has benefited from their findings.

—*S. M. Alexanyan and V. I. Krivshesiko*

Brother Joseph, if you will permit it, and say the word, I will have you out of this prison in five hours, if the jail has to come down to do it.

—John Taylor

These days one of the worst things you can be accused of is good intentions.

—Michael Kinsley

Nothing is more annoying than a friend who is always late.

—Clay Dickinson

If you never tell your secret to your friend, you will never fear him when he becomes your enemy.

—Menander

In prosperity our friends know us; in adversity we know our friends.

—Churton Collins

Hand grasps at hand, eye lights eye in good friendship.

—Robert Browning

I see no comfort in outliving one's friends, and remaining a mere monument of the times which are past.

—Thomas Jefferson

Greater love hath no man than this, that a man lay down his life for his friends.

—Jesus Christ

One of the best things in my life is being friends with the six- and seven-year-olds I coach in soccer. That is the age when they are drinking in life, and they never dry up.

—Jim Jardine

Remembrance, like a candle, burns brightest at Christmas.

—Charles Dickens

Believing, hear what you deserve to hear;
    Your birthday as my own to me is dear.
But yours gives most; for mine did only lend me to the world;
    Yours gave to me a friend.

—Martial

Practice random kindness and senseless acts of beauty." We're not sure exactly where the phrase started, . . . but it seems to be gradually spreading across our country. One man describes it in these words: "Anything nice or good that you think should be done, do it randomly."

Examples: A woman drives up to the toll booth to go across a bridge and pays for the next six cars behind her. Imagine what each driver must feel when the collection attendant tells them that nice lady has paid for their crossing.

A man went into the school in a depressed area and painted several classrooms which needed it badly. He left hot meals on kitchen tables in the poor part of town. He slipped money into a proud old woman's purse.

In New Jersey a dozen people got together and cleaned an old couple's apartment from top to bottom as the couple looked on. A teenager in Chicago cleaned the snow off his family's driveway, and then went across the street and cleaned the driveway of a neighbor. A woman planted flowers beside a roadway. A man scrubbed graffiti from a park bench.

Acts of kindness all, random acts of beauty. But senseless? No. Wonderful? Yes!

—Bill Ziegler

FIELD OF DREAMS

I believe the human mind is like a field in the spring of the year. That field doesn't talk back to you to say, "Plant on my back, cotton or corn or rice." It doesn't care what you plant; but whatever you plant and fertilize and water, that is what you are going to gather at harvest time. So if you plant in your mind: "I can't borrow this money," and "This project is going to be a failure," well, that is what grows in your mind.

—Wallace E. Johnson

We have it in our power to begin the world again.

—Thomas Paine

To GET HERE

START HERE!

—From the Wall Street Journal

Why keep up with the Joneses when there are ways today to avoid them altogether? Keeping up with the Joneses isn't taken so seriously these days. It's trying to keep up with those baby boomers in the small hotel on our cul-de-sac.

—Marvin K. Gardner

Carrying little Kunta in his strong arms, [Omoro] walked to the edge of the village, lifted his baby up with his face to the heavens, and said softly, *"Fend kiling dorong leh warrata ka iteh tee."* (Behold—the only thing greater than yourself.)

—*Alex Haley*

It is easy in the world to live after the world's opinion; it is easy in solitude to live after our own; but the great man is he who in the midst of the crowd keeps with perfect sweetness the independence of solitude.

—*Ralph Waldo Emerson*

Even more pure,
As tempted more; more able to endure,
As more exposed to suffering and distress;
Thence, also, more alive to tenderness.

—*William Wordsworth*

There will be times and places when our sense of personal responsibility will be tried, for we live in a world which is in constant conspiracy against the brave. It is an age-old struggle, the roar of the crowd on one side and the voice of your conscience on the other.

—*Douglas MacArthur*

Get someone else to blow your horn and the sound will carry twice as far.

—*Will Rogers*

We strolled about everwhere through the broad, straight, level streets, and enjoyed the pleasant strangeness of a city [Salt Lake City] of fifteen thousand inhabitants with no loafers perceptible in it; and no visible drunkards or noisy people; . . . and a grand general air of neatness, repair, thrift and comfort, around and about and over the whole. And everywhere were workshops, factories, and all manner of industries; and intent faces and busy hands were to be seen wherever one looked; and in one's ears was the ceaseless clink of hammers, the buzz of trade and the contented hum of drums and fly-wheels.

—Mark Twain

[The] West's old traditional promise—that, if you can get there, you may have a new beginning, regardless of bloodlines or station in life—is most likely to be kept.

—Stanley W. Cloud

Filming can take a lot out of you. Gardening puts it back. Its rewards are many. Its bountiful beauty nourishes my body and soul.

—Richard Dysart

Let us build houses that restore to man the life-giving, life-enhancing elements of nature.

—Frank Lloyd Wright

What it does [living in a Wright house] is fill the need for a gentle purging of the soul provided by something simple, natural and beautiful. . . . It is like living with a great and quiet soul. Some of its peace and calm carries over to you.

—*Loren Pope*

Architecture's genius, in a career that spanned seven decades, Frank Lloyd Wright invented new houses for our democracy and changed the way we lived. He did not look to old Europe, the acropolis, or any time in the past: He was a steadfast American . . . who thought the future was in the country's own nourishing soil.

—*Joseph Giovannini*

One of my favorite places in the world: My friend's house. A place to relax. The view is of her own vineyards. . . . Privacy. Profound seclusion. No incoming phone calls. None. What I feel here is simply this: at ease. There are other good points, too. A serious kitchen garden. Big collection of jazz. . . . Books I want to read. . . . A dog that goes back and forth with her. She has everything, including nonchalance.

We're middle-aged. We're finally at peace. It's wonderful.

—*J. Peterman*

So give your melons time to bask in the noonday sun.

—*Wayne B. Lynn*

Early composers in the Church were eager to have the restored gospel expressed through music. . . . It is difficult to find music that is more effective than the hymns. The familiarity of the hymn works in its favor to warm the hearts of the people. We respond to that which is familiar. We are a church of choirs. Through effective use of hymns, singers can foster spirituality.

—*Michael F. Moody*

May I share with you one of the principles that governs my life? It is the realization that what I receive I must pass on to others. The knowledge that I have acquired must not remain imprisoned in my brain. I owe it to many men and women to do something with it. I feel the need to pay back what was given to me. Call it gratitude.

Isn't this what education is all about?

—*Elie Wiesel*

Before becoming a U.S. citizen, I was an immigrant of Dutch-Indonesian descent. When I arrived in this country, I did not find any support group or organization to help me with a job or counseling. I was expected to cope with the situation and adapt as well as could be done.

There may lie the answer to some of our country's problems. Instead of seeing Asian, Polynesian, and Eastern European immigrants or blacks and Hispanics, we should only see Americans and future Americans.

—*F. J. Kohlschein*

I labored as hard as any man could.

—*Truman O. Angell*

I've been teaching the members in Hong Kong that it doesn't matter whether you are of Western or Eastern culture, but that the Church has its own culture. It's the Church culture—its principles and programs—that we need to follow.

—*Tai, Kwok Yuen*

In leaving Salt Lake City and Utah I shall carry away with me pleasant memories of the Saints as an honest, industrious and God-fearing people, who have done great things for the amelioration of mankind and who have made a desert to blossom like a rose.

—*H. R. Harper*

As long as we keep dancing, we'll remember who we are.

—*Cheyenne Indian*

You can no more force the Spirit to respond than you can force a bean to sprout, or an egg to hatch before its time. You can create a climate to foster growth; you can nourish, and protect; but you cannot force or compel: You must await the growth.

—*Boyd K. Packer*

Nations die. Old regions grow arid, or suffer other change. Resilient man picks up his tools and his arts, and moves on, taking his memories with him.

—*Will Durant*

Your problems begin first in your own heart. . . . Earnestly seek the Lord. . . .

More than all else, your sincere humility and great courage to look into your own heart and turn the key found therein will inspire others to look inwardly and turn the key in their hearts.

—Stephen R. Covey

Cast not away therefore your confidence, which hath great recompense of reward.

For ye have need of patience, that, after ye have done the will of God, ye might receive the promise.

For yet a little while, and he that shall come will come.

—Paul

Music is a moral law. It gives a soul to the universe, wings to the mind, flight to the imagination, a charm to sadness, gaiety and life to everything. It is the essence of order, and leads to all that is good, just, and beautiful, of which it is the invisible, but nevertheless dazzling, passionate, and eternal form.

—Plato

Speaking personally, I know of no single activity that has affected my life more than coming to know intimately the words of the Lord and then attempting to conform my life to them.

—Gene R. Cook

The study of the doctrines of the gospel will improve behavior quicker than a study of behavior will improve behavior. Preoccupation with unworthy behavior can lead to unworthy behavior.

—Boyd K. Packer

There are certain blessings obtained when one searches the scriptures. As a person studies the words of the Lord and obeys them, he or she draws closer to the Savior and obtains a greater desire to live a righteous life. The power to resist temptation increases, and spiritual weaknesses are overcome. Spiritual wounds are healed.

—Merrill J. Bateman

Many have . . . resigned themselves to accept the wickedness and cruelty of the world as being irreparable. They have given up hope. They have decided to quit trying to make the world a better place in which they and their families can live. They have surrendered to despair.

. . . But regardless of this dark picture, which will ultimately get worse, we must never allow ourselves to give up hope! . . .

To all who have harbored feelings of despair and an absence of hope, I offer the words of the Lord through the Prophet Joseph Smith: "Fear not, little flock; do good; let earth and hell combine against you, for if ye are built upon my rock, they cannot prevail. . . .

"Look unto me in every thought; doubt not, fear not" (D&C 6:34, 36), "even so am I in the midst of you" (D&C 6:32).

—M. Russell Ballard

To go on forever and fail and go on again,
And be mauled to the earth and arise, . . .
With the half of a broken hope for a pillow at night
That somehow the right is the right
And the smooth shall bloom from the rough.

—*Robert Louis Stevenson*

Never despair. But if you do, work on in despair.

—*Edmund Burke*

Master of human destinies am I. . . .
I knock unbidden once at every gate!
If sleeping, wake—if feasting, rise before
I turn away. It is the hour of fate . . .
Seek me in vain and uselessly implore—
I answer not, and I return no more.

—*John James Ingalls*

The only way to know real joy and permanent satisfaction is to
fail in reaching something that is beyond us rather than succeed
in doing something that lies within our reach. . . . The happy
people are those who fail in striving to reach the mountain tops;
the unhappy people are those who are content to camp at points
which are easily reached.

—*Raymond Calkins*

Man comes a pilgrim of the universe,
Out of the mysteries that were before. . . .
His feet have felt the pressure of old worlds,
And are to tread on others yet unnamed—
Worlds sleeping yet in some new dream of God.

—Edwin Markham

The diminution or withdrawal of the Spirit, the spiritual dry
spells, and spiritual deserts we face are not always due to our
unworthiness or to our failure. I am convinced they are part of
our mortal trial and the will of the Lord. . . . Prove yourself
devoted even when [left] in the realms of solitude.

—Truman G. Madsen

Set goals and follow through on them. You transform yourself
from one of life's spectators into a real participant.

—Lou Holtz

We want young men entering the mission field who can enter
"on the run."

—Ezra Taft Benson

To find my one sentence, concise, as if hammered in metal. Not
to enchant anybody. Not to earn a lasting name in posterity. An
unnamed need for order, for rhythm, for form, which three
words are opposed to chaos and nothingness.

—Czeslaw Milostz

'll never forget where I came from and how I got here. Besides, looking back on my own life, I'd say that the secret is not to be without anger but to focus it and generate creative energy from it.

—Robert Guillaume

he human capacity for decency and goodness, even under the most adverse and forbidding of circumstances, can be extraordinarily edifying.

—Robert Coles

o give life a meaning one must have a purpose larger than oneself.

—Will Durant

his team [Chicago Bulls] deserved to be booed. I've never sat through an exhibition of basketball like that in my life. And I'd better never again, either.

—Phil Jackson (coach)

he LDS athletes in Puno [Peru] are gracious in both victory and defeat. Their sportsmanship helps build unity with their friends and neighbors of other friends.

—Melvin Leavitt

To love is morally superior than to doubt, a good heart more to be valued than a razor-sharp mind. Shakespeare and Milton subscribe to the same priority of heart to mind.

—*John S. Tanner*

To learn to see with one's soul must be like gaining that dimension of compensating senses that comes to the blind. Suddenly questions like "where is my universe? where is my world?" pop up. One's purpose in life is redefined.

—*William Leach*

I am an American because this Nation has no scheme or plan of conquest, because it has a respect for the rights of other peoples and of other nations, because it promotes justice and honor in the relationships of nations, because it loves the ways of peace as against war.

—*J. Reuben Clark, Jr.*

Bashing our politicians and our public thinkers on almost any subject—religion, racism, abortion, environment included— gives rise to further argument. Who do the people of the press— including those who write letters to the editors—think they are? The old adage seems to hold here: that unless you've walked in another man's mocassins . . . or look to the beam in your own eye first . . . there is no room for idle talk, let alone judgment.

—*Kelly M. Rhinelander*

Just say it was slippery out there. . . . I wouldn't want to jeopardize my shoe contract.

—Karl Malone (Utah Jazz)

If you believe in your dreams, there's no limit to what you can do.

—Sam Walton

Build thee more stately mansions, O my soul!

—Oliver Wendell Holmes

Got troubles and crashing disappointment? Radical change? Dream a new dream! God has provided rich options.

—James Quayle Cannon

OVERTIME

Time is a great teacher.

—*Carl Sandburg*

Just remember, once you're over the hill you begin to pick up speed.

—*Charles Schulz*

William Saroyan wrote a great play on the theme that purity of heart is the one success worth having. "In the time of your life, live." That time is short and it doesn't return again. It is slipping away while I write this and while you read it, and monosyllable of the clock is loss, loss, loss, unless you devote your heart to its opposition.

—*Tennessee Williams*

When we are young, we sometimes behave as if there were no tomorrow. . . .

. . . Conduct your life today so your tomorrows are not burdened with bad or embarrassing memories.

—*Dallin H. Oaks*

Eternity is the extension—not the replacement—of the patterns of this earth.

—*Truman G. Madsen*

Life is eating us up. We shall be fables presently.

—*Ralph Waldo Emerson*

It is possible that only human beings, of all living species, do not live entirely in the present.

—*Isaac Asimov*

I love life! The potential for good far outweighs the potential for bad. And I have faith in people.

—*David O. McKay*

One's old age should be tranquil, as childhood should be playful. Hard work at either extremity of life seems out of place.

—*Matthew Arnold*

Seniors should avoid falling into ruts. Variety, variety, variety. Change, change, change. People get tired because of boredom.

—*Jack LaLaine*

Contrary to popular notions about the young and the old, nowadays it is voters over fifty who are the agents of political change in America.

—*Andrew Kohut*

I believe that we should stay fit both physically and spiritually. Christ said that my body is a temple of God, and so I try to keep it healthy through exercise.

—*Placido Melo*

When I was younger, I felt everyone at sixty should be shot. Now I've changed my mind—and a few of my habits.

—*Ringo Starr*

There aren't enough hours in the day for baby boomers to live their lives. . . . We've shifted prime time to a full hour earlier.

—*Harry Fuller*

I speak to you as a teacher and a student—one is both, always. I also speak to you as a witness.

I speak to you, for I do not want my past to become your future.

—*Elie Wiesel*

I'm not promoting miracle cures. Eat better, exercise, get enough sleep—and you will feel better.

—*Jay Kordich*

Instead of the watch customarily presented at retirement parties, many people nearing the age of Social Security these days might wish for a high-powered calculator.

They have a lot of complicated computations to perform before they decide such questions as when to start drawing Social Security benefits and whether to keep working at either full-time or part-time jobs.

—*Chet Currier*

What endures? Quality. Reality. Change.

—*Ron Javers*

History with its flickering lamp stumbles along the trail of the past, trying to reconstruct its scenes, to revive its echoes, and kindle with pale gleams the passion of former days.

—*Winston Churchill*

The biggest change among people who will be retiring in the twenty-first century is their belief that the Social Security will not be there to do much for them.

—*Bill Chapman*

How can you prepare for a retirement that can last longer than the years spent working?

—Paul Allen

There is more to life than increasing its speed.

—Mohandas K. Gandhi

Human beings can alter their lives by altering their attitudes of mind.

—William James

The issue . . . , as always, is whether opportunites are fully employed—opportunities for the fullest realization of our capacities, so that we become our best. . . .

. . . Though opportunities knock more than once, we cannot put them off with too much indecisive procrastination. . . .

In this great free land of America, and in our beloved Church, opportunities come unlimited, but only to those who, "If sleeping, wake—if feasting, rise . . ."

—Obert C. Tanner

So many of us are afraid to leave our "comfort zones" and thus cheat ourselves of some of the greatest adventures of our lives.

—Robert L. Backman

Come, my friends,
'Tis not too late to seek a newer world.

—Alfred, Lord Tennyson

In the pursuit of values we discover that life is within, not outside us.

—Lowell L. Bennion

The charge of oneself is the root of all other charges.

—Confucius

What though the radiance which was once so bright
Be now forever taken from my sight,
Though nothing can bring back the hour
Of splendor in the grass, of glory in the flower;
We will grieve not, rather find
Strength in what remains behind;
In the primal sympathy
Which having been must ever be;
In the soothing thoughts that spring
Out of human suffering;
In the faith that looks through death,
In years that bring the philosophic mind.

—William Wordsworth

I think the necessity of being *ready* increases.—Look to it.

—*Abraham Lincoln*

I can no other answer make but thanks,
And thanks, and ever thanks.

—*William Shakespeare*

Let me not look back in anger, not forward in fear, but around in awareness.

—*James Thurber*

Most of us have collections of sayings we live by. . . .
Whenever words fly up at me from the printed page as I read, I intercept them instantly, knowing they are for me. I turn them over carefully in my mind and cling to them hard.

—*David Grayson*

No man is wise enough by himself.

—*Plautus*

Time heals our griefs and quarrels, because we change; we are not the same individuals we were.

—*Blaise Pascal*

Who is a wise man? He who learns of all men.

—*From the Talmud*

How a person looks at the affairs of life determines one's gladness or sadness. A matter of pessimism or optimism.

—*Ward J. Roylance*

Upon joining a singing class . . . , [the professor] tried and tried in vain to teach me when ten years of age to run the scale or carry a simple tune and finally gave up in despair. He said that I could never, in this world, learn to sing. . . .

When I was about twenty-five years of age, [another professor] informed me that I could sing, but added, "I would like to be at least forty miles away while you are doing it." . . .

I am pleased to be able to say that I can now sing with piano or organ accompaniment. . . .

. . . It required a vast amount of practice to learn, and my first hymn was sung many hundreds of times before I succeeded in getting it right.

—*Heber J. Grant*

I have learned, in whatsoever state I am, therewith to be content.

—*Paul*

When you're coming up to seventy, you take an inventory of your life and you tend to reflect a little more, having arrived at the mastery of some kind of odiom. I would far rather take a master class in guitar from Segóvia when he was eighty than when he was twenty-five.

—*James Dickey*

When I get time
I'll regulate my life
In such a way that I may get
Acquainted with my wife.

—*Thomas L. Marson*

Life cannot make me treasure weeds;
    I love each moment's flower.
Nor do I feed on future's needs;
    But feast on the present hour.

—*Eugene G. E. Botelho*

EMPOWERED

Neglect not the gift that is in thee, which was given thee by prophecy, with the laying on of the hands.

—Paul

[We face the] challenge of choosing our heroes and examples wisely, while also giving thanks for those legions of friends and citizens who are not so famous but who are "no less service-able" than the Moronis of our lives.

—Howard W. Hunter

The respect of another is the first restoration of the self-respect a man has lost; our ideal of what he is becomes to him the hope and pattern of what he may become.

—Henry Drummond

There are two things needed in these days; first, for rich men to find out how poor men live; and second, for the poor men to know how rich men work.

—Edward Atkinson

If a man does not exercise his arm he develops no bicep muscle; and if a man does not exercise his soul, he acquires no muscle in his soul, no strength of character, no vigor of moral fiber, nor beauty of spiritual growth.

—Henry Drummond

You can't build a reputation on what you are going to do.

—Henry Ford

Nothing is at last sacred but the integrity of your own mind. Absolve you to yourself and you shall have the suffrage of the world.

—Ralph Waldo Emerson

If you do not magnify your callings, God will hold you responsible for those whom you might have saved had you done your duty.

—John Taylor

Power corrupts the few, while weakness corrupts the many.

—Eric Hoffer

No sadder proof can be given by a man of his own littleness than disbelief in great men.

—Thomas Carlyle

When we begin to lose hope, we are faltering also in our measure of faith.

—M. Russell Ballard

Labour to keep alive in your breast that little spark of celestial fire, called conscience.

—George Washington

The moment of greatest danger is when there is so little light that darkness seems normal. . . . We must remember . . . it is not necessary, either, that Satan extinguish our light, if he can simply keep it dim.

—Neal A. Maxwell

That we have so little faith is not sad, but that we have so little faithfulness.

—Henry David Thoreau

You don't have to blow out the other fellow's light to let your own shine, you know.

—*Bernard M. Paruch*

We are doing our best to fulfill the duties and responsibilities thereof [as Presiding Bishop], to exercise judgment, accuracy and economy in all the matters entrusted to our care; and to see that honesty and integrity are maintained in every department of the work. While the duties and labors are many and diverse, we are endeavoring to so organize and systematize the affairs that every phase of the work is carried forth promptly and thoroughly. I do enjoy this work.

—*Sylvester Q. Cannon*

Some people are weak in their faith and testimonies but are not even aware of how precarious their situation is. Many of them likely would be offended at the suggestion. They raise their right hand to sustain Church leaders and then murmur and complain when a decision does not square with their way of thinking. They claim to be obedient to God's commandments but do not feel at all uncomfortable about purchasing food at the store on Sunday and then asking the Lord to bless it. Some say they would give their lives for the Lord, yet they refuse to serve in the nursery.

—*Joseph B. Wirthlin*

Obedience brings faith. It brings forth the blessings of heaven. Disobedience brings forth heartache and despair.

—*L. Tom Perry*

Live your religion devotedly. True happiness and joy and satisfaction will come out of that commitment, for the gospel is true. I have seen it in my own life and in the experiences I have had. If you want really to be happy, then simply live the gospel.

—*Joseph Anderson*

For some, the self-discovery that results in having their handwriting analyzed becomes a necessary catalyst for change.

—*J. J. Leonard*

If the people of all the nations of the earth will repent, turn unto him [the Lord], and obey his commandments, . . . they should receive the Holy Ghost.

—*Orson Pratt*

Remember, luck is opportunity meeting up with preparation, so you must prepare yourself to be lucky.

—*Gregory Hines*

Yet I argue not
Against Heav'n's hand or will, nor bate
    one jot
Of heart or hope; but still bear up, and
    steer
Right onward.

—*John Milton*

I am not far within the mark when I say that all the armies that ever marched, and all the navies that ever were built, and all the parliaments that ever sat, and all the kings that ever reigned, put together, have not afflicted the life of man upon this earth as powerfully as has that one solitary life [i.e., of Jesus Christ].

—James A. Francis

When I was a student in college I returned by train one night from a football game. As I left the train a grown man, intoxicated and helpless, fell from the train step and into a gutter. One of my associates said, "Let the bum lie there." I happened to know that he was one of the ablest citizens in that community. But able or not able, known or unknown, I quickly picked him up, placed him in a taxicab, and sent him home. I never drank in my life and I have no use of intoxicants. I despise them. But it is not in my heart to despise the man who is under the influence of liquor. There are those who think I am wrong, but I hope I may continue to feel as I do.

—Albert Buchner Coe

I am very proud to be the descendant of the man who so profoundly changed the history of humanity.

—Crisobal Colon
(direct descendant of Columbus)

Academicians characterize teachings as a "load," whereas research is called an "opportunity." We are not raided for our teachers.

—Arthur Smith

I've had the privilege of spending my lifetime with the best men in the world [the Brethren of the Church]. I have loved them, and they have loved me. One of the greatest blessings the Lord has granted me is friendship of good and noble men. Each one has greatly influenced my life for good, not only because of what he has said or done or achieved, but because of what he is personally.

—Joseph Anderson

What's a drunken man like . . . ?
    Like a drown'd man, a fool, and a madman: one draught above heat makes him a fool; the second mads him; and a third drowns him.

—William Shakespeare

He who would lead must first himself be led; who would be loved be capable to love . . . and being honored, honor what's above: This know the men who leave the world their names.

—Bayard Taylor

If human beings are to progress, if we are to continue our long, brutal, heartbreaking journey out of the caves and swamps, then the way must be led by those who are not afraid of the dark.

—Pete Hamill

Prove all things; hold fast that which is good.
    Abstain from all appearance of evil.

—Paul

Alcoholism should be studied by every youth before he takes a first drink. Among many advantages of knowing in advance the hazards that lie ahead, there is an understanding to be gained toward those who are so afflicted.

—Obert C. Tanner

Greatness of any kind has no greater foe than the habit of drinking.

—Walter Scott

Every man has an image of himself which fails in one way or another with reality. It's the size of the discrepancy between illusion and reality that matters.

—John Homer Miller

If you would not be forgotten, either write things worth reading or do things worth writing.

—Benjamin Franklin

An expert is a man from out of town who blows in, blows off, and blows out.

—Aldon Joseph Anderson

May the outward and inward man be at one.

—Socrates

The greatest thing that would break my heart is if I got *there* and could not do the job for the American people.

—Ross Perot

I know today that [for] those of us who are spared, every day we live, we live with the grace of God. I hit a bottom that I hope not many people have to experience. . . . [I] have learned what a miracle is. I have learned what love is. I have learned to accept God in my life. Today I reach out on a daily basis, not so much to ask for help, but to offer help. That's my life.

—Harry Reems
(reformed alcoholic)

God created man in his own image, in the image of God created he him.

—Genesis 1:27

There are three marks of a superior man: being virtuous, he is free from anxiety; being wise, he is free from perplexity; being brave, he is free from fear.

—Confucius

The epochs are discerned by the types of people who lead them.

—Heinrich Mann

An expert is one who knows less and less about more and more.

—Aldon Joseph Anderson

My daily employment and my Sunday activities are wrapped in the Church. In making an evaluation of my personal growth, I decided I needed to broaden and build my life, so I took piano lessons.

—Mark Hurst

RED INK

Will ye also go away?

—Jesus Christ

America is great because America is good, and if America ever ceases to be good, America will cease to be great.

—Alexis de Tocqueville

And thus we see the end of him who perverteth the ways of the Lord; and thus we see that the devil will not support his children at the last day, but doth speedily drag them down to hell.

—Mormon

All of our personal experience confirms the fact that we must endure personal suffering in the process of repentance.

—Dallin H. Oaks

[Personal] suffering is a very important part of repentance. One has not begun to repent until he has suffered intensely for his sins. . . . If a person hasn't suffered, he hasn't repented.

—Spencer W. Kimball

We see about us constant change. Even the pace of life itself has speeded up. Sometimes it seems that the world is undergoing such throes of change that people are disoriented, not knowing what is of value. Right and wrong, however, are as they always were. The principles of the gospel are unaltered. All of men's evil speaking and all of men's evil acting cannot alter one jot or tittle of the commandments of God.

—Spencer W. Kimball

I have been deceived [regarding the Mormons].

—Ulysses S. Grant
(while visiting Utah, 1875)

Don't let them push your [anger] button. The one trying to get you angry wants to control you.

—Gerald I. Nierinberg

It is best not to be angry; and best in the next place, to be quickly reconciled.

—Samuel Johnson

The nearer you come in relation with a person, the more necessary tact and courtesy become.

—Oliver Wendell Holmes

Never tell a lie; but the truth you don't have to tell.

—George Safir

Inevitably, anytime we are too vulnerable, we feel the need to protect ourselves from further wounds. So we resort to sarcasm, cutting humor, criticism—anything that will keep from exposing the tenderness within. Each partner tends to wait on the initiative of the other for love, only to be disappointed, but also confirmed as to the rightness of the accusations made.

—Stephen R. Covey

The only thing he stands for is the national anthem.

—Bill Yates

Nothing in life is so exhilarating as to be shot at without result.

—Winston Churchill

Folks who neglect history are doomed to relive it—and its mistakes.

—Jack Goodman

Struggle for power is the essence of history.

—Kenneth C. Davis

Secret of my success? I have a special chute that goes down to the Potomac—anyone who crosses [me] will be flushed down the chute. Actually, I do all I can to provide the federal funding to reinvigorate this country.

—Robert Byrd

Most folks eventually can see the handwriting on the wall, although most of them continue to insist that it is addressed to someone else.

—Reverend Reeve

Life is not a sound bite.

—Public Broadcasting Service

Don't take steroids! The risks are not worth the gains.

—Michael Oshid

Darby Checketts is the kind of man who describes himself as a "Human Post-It note," a man who goes to a production of Shakespeare's "Henry V" and sees it as "a marvelous study in leadership."

—Jerry Johnston

It's that primal wish in all of us not to be tied by gravity, to be that curious soul above it all. Through the years, however, I have learned an important lesson: If you're gonna fly, you're gonna encounter turbulence.

—Richard Bach

Our youthful years are frequently a kind of Kirtland—Lifting us to high mountain peaks where the vision is clear. But sooner or later we have our Nauvoos—frozen rivers and parched deserts to cross, a moral or financial or intellectual wilderness to tame. It will not always be fun.

—Bruce C. Hafen

I conceive that a great part of the miseries of mankind are brought upon them by the false estimates they have made of the value of things.

—Benjamin Franklin

You will have all kinds of trials to pass through. And it is quite as necessary for you to be tried as it was for Abraham and other men of God, and God will feel after you, and He will take hold of you and wrench your very heart strings, and if you cannot stand it you will not be fit for an inheritance in the Celestial Kingdom of God.

—Joseph Smith

The two hardest things to handle in life are failure and success.

—*Franklin S. Richards*

A deep distress hath humanized my soul.

—*William Wordsworth*

For it had been better for them not to have known the way of righteousness, than, after they have known it, to turn from the holy commandment delivered unto them.

—*Peter*

The forces of good are clearly and continually under attack. There are times when it seems the world is almost drowning in a flood of filth and degradation. And I want to cry out, "Hold on! Hold on to what is right and true." Therein is safety. Don't let yourself be swept away.

—*Spencer W. Kimball*

Income tax returns are the most imaginative fiction being written today.

—*Herman Wouk*

Awake, my soul! No longer droop in sin. Rejoice, O my heart.

—*Nephi*

HIGH YIELD

Each of us boys learned the work ethic from our father, working side by side with him in his auto body shop. Repairing auto bodies is tough work and close work for a family. If a fight broke out among us, we'd take it home and settle it around the dinner table, where Mother taught us the art of negotiation based on gospel principles.

—Bill Hansen, Jr.

People tend to underestimate the challenge success brings. Good people draw closer to the Lord through adversity *and* success.

—S. Lynn Richards

We work for many reasons. Generally, the most immediate reason is to feed, clothe, and house ourselves and the ones we love. But work also gives us an opportunity to develop and practice skills and talents. . . .

Work discloses something essential about human identity and dignity that transcends time and culture.

—Steven Epperson

The best way out is always through.

—Robert Frost

[The Savior] taught, "Behold it is my will that you shall pay all your debts" (D&C 104:78). Yes, even if it takes years, pay your debts.

—James M. Paramore

Perhaps of all the creations of man, language is the most astonishing.

—Lytton Strachey

Of all the words of tongue and pen,
The saddest are these: "It might have been!"

—Author unknown

In general those who have nothing to say contrive to spend the longest time in doing it.

—James Russell Lowell

Live to learn, learn to love, and you'll love to live.

—Matthew Cowley

Write the things which ye have seen and heard, save it be those which are forbidden. . . .

For behold, out of the books which have been written, and which shall be written, shall this people be judged, for by them shall their works be known unto men.

—Jesus Christ

Be strong and of a good courage.

—Joshua 1:6

Patience is tied very closely to . . . faith . . . in our Heavenly Father and Jesus Christ. When we are unduly impatient with circumstances, we may be suggesting that we know what is best—better than does God. Or, at least, we are asserting that our timetable is better than His. Either way, we are questioning the reality of God's omniscience.

—Neal A. Maxwell

These people [the Indians of Hispaniola] love their neighbours as themselves; their discourse is ever sweet and gentle, accompanied by a smile. I swear to Your Majesties, there is not in the world a better nation or a better land.

—Christopher Columbus

Sanctify yourselves: for tomorrow the Lord will do wonders among you.

—Joshua

I know that which the Lord hath commanded me, and I glory in it. I do not glory of myself, but I glory in that which the Lord hath commanded me; yea, and this is my glory, that perhaps I may be an instrument in the hands of God to bring some soul to repentance; and this is my joy.

—Alma

What's needed is a vision of an America that works with all of its vital organs ticking and all of its citizens participating.

—Arthur Fletcher

Even more pure,
As tempted more; more able to endure,
As more exposed to suffering and distress;
Thence, also, more alive to tenderness.

—William Wordsworth

The banker, the lawyer, and the politician are still our best bets for a laugh. Audiences haven't changed at all, and neither have the three above professions.

—Will Rogers

Readers of the Book of Mormon can appreciate the remarkable achievements represented by a democratic government among the Nephites. Principles of religious tolerance, popular sovereignty, accountability of leaders, and the rule of law are all embodied in this combination.

—Kendall Stiles

Everybody really knows what to do to have his life filled with joy. What is it? Quit hating people; start liking them. Quit doing wrong, quit being filled with fear. Quit thinking about yourself and go out and do something for other people.

—Norman Vincent Peale

One reported encounter at Versailles shortly after the American revolutionary war involved the ambassador from Britain, a French minister, and Benjamin Franklin from the United States. The British ambassador raised his glass in a toast to King George III, who, he said, like the sun, cast the beneficent and warming glow of his splendid countenance across the earth. The French minister toasted Louis XVI, who, he said, like the moon, cast the beneficent and blessed light of his countenance across the world. Benjamin Franklin slowly stood and toasted George Washington, who, he said, like Joshua of old, commanded the sun and the moon to stand still, and they did.

—Marion D. Hanks

It is well for the heart to be naive, and for the mind not to be.

—Anatole France

You can't often compare painters with writers, because of the apples-and-oranges problem of imagining links between dissimilar arts. But in the case of Rembrandt van Rijn you can, and the temptation to do it, if not carried too far, can hardly be resisted. He was the Shakespeare of seventeenth-century painting.

—Robert Hughes

All these other departments really work. But art, that's fun. And why should we pay people more if they are having fun?

—Tony Smith

Reality Ad. Join the FBI: Just pick up your phone; we're already on the line.

—John Mauren

And the heart that is soonest awake to the flowers—is always the first to be touched by the thorns.

—Thomas Moore

Had we ourselves no faults, we should find less pleasure discovering them in others.

—François de La Rochefoucauld

School thy feelings; there is power
In the cool, collected mind.

—Charles W. Penrose

Your aim is not to get ahead of others but to surpass yourself; to begin today to be the person you want to be; to immortalize today and all the tomorrows that lie ahead, in order that your life may have eternal significance. Cultivate an unquenchable appetite for learning.

—Hugh B. Brown

Learn by experience—other people's if possible.

—Bruce Barton

Be not angry that you cannot make others as you wish them to be, since you cannot make yourself as you wish to be.

—Thomas à Kempis

We cannot escape history. . . . No personal significance, or insignificance, can spare one or another of us. The fiery trial through which we pass, will light us down, in honor or dishonor, to the latest generation.

—Abraham Lincoln

Is it *really* important to save a lizard in the California desert dunes? . . . Kill off the species, scientists say, and we may lose a cure for a disease or a clue about how to improve our lives. The essential ingredients for many medicines—including those that treat Hodgkin's disease and childhood leukemia—are derived from species once thought to serve no purpose.

—*Randy Fitzgerald*

Scare mongers have always underestimated human ingenuity.

—*From an editorial in the* Wall Street Journal

There's no such thing as guaranteed return on anything these days.

—*John S. Demott*

Governments too often prefer top-down strategies such as subsidies for prestige, plant rehab or relocation. The benches in the trenches matter more than an executive directive.

—*W. Ferguson*

Work is what keeps people young. . . . We should have an ambition, we should have a desire to work to the full extent of our ability. Working eight or nine hours a day has never injured me, and I do not believe it will injure anyone else.

—*Heber J. Grant*

Work is pleasing to the Lord.

—Heber J. Grant

There is one thing we can do and the happiest people are those who do it to the limit of their ability. We can be completely present. We can be all there. We can control the tendency of our minds to wander from the situation we are in toward yesterday, toward tomorrow, toward something we have forgotten, toward some other place we are going next. It is hard to do this, but it is harder to understand afterward wherein it was we fell so short. It was where and when we ceased to give our entire attention to the person, the opportunity before us.

—Mark Van Doren

I have learned that the periods between challenges are extremely restful, but there is no growth. You grow when you are being challenged.

—John B. Dickson

Humility gives us a proper perspective in the vastness of God's creation. . . . Being mindful of shortcomings is a necessary condition of personal progress.

—Obert C. Tanner

O, the difference of man and man!

—William Shakespeare

Life needs a menu. Novels, biographies, help; but nothing is better than a good atlas.

An atlas tells you which river you must go down, or up, next and which far country you must go to *someday*.

—J. Peterman

Long-time friend and supporter John Crean told me, "Dig the hole, Bob," when I called to tell Crean I was going to cancel the project [building the Crystal Cathedral] when construction costs nearly doubled.

—Robert Schuller

Mother, come see this blaze [of the burning laboratory]. . . . You'll not soon see another so spectacular.

—Thomas A. Edison

When you work for the Lord the retirement benefits are out of this world.

—Harry Gibbons

All those who do not agree, signify by saying "I resign."

—C.E.O.

There is no greatness where there is not simplicity.

—Leo Tolstoi

THINK TANK

Think of these things: whence you came, where you are going, and to whom you must account.

—*Benjamin Franklin*

I have sworn upon the altar of God eternal hostility against every form of tyranny over the mind of man.

—*Thomas Jefferson*

It seems to me that a tremendous amount of dough should go to things of life instead of things of death; we have to eliminate the gap between the haves and have-nots. We have to think in fresh terms now.

—*Studs Terkel*

The unleashed power of the atom has changed everything save our modes of thinking.

—*Albert Einstein*

Before you do anything, think of God, that his light may precede your energies.

—*Sextus the Pythagorean*

As a missionary, you will have times when you will be influenced by the Holy Spirit when you write or speak. You may write words you do not recognize and say words you didn't know you knew. You will silently marvel at the privilege of knowing that you are being especially blessed for the Lord's purposes. People will believe your words because you will give them by the power of the Holy Ghost. You must be pure and positively clean; you must be sharp in your preparation, communication skills, and gospel knowledge.

—Ed J. Pinegar

Joy such as is not known in any other work comes to them [missionaries], and there comes too a personal development that will be of benefit to them no matter what their future occupations may be. . . .

I can speak from knowledge,—that there is no joy equal to that which comes to the man or woman who is performing missionary labor.

—Melvin J. Ballard

Great knowledge carries with it great responsibility, a fact often ignored by modern pundits.

—Jean-François Revel

If man understood the enigmas of life, there would be no need for the arts.

—Jack Lemmon

Hitler, who considered himself an artist, believed art had to reflect conventional ideas of beauty and nobility. Modern art is about individual expression and reflects the view that each person sees the world in a different way, that no one perception of reality can be accepted as an absolute truth. The Nazis knew they had to crush that idea in order to survive.

—Christoph Stalzl

God does not die on the day when we cease to believe in a personal deity; but we die on the day when our lives cease to be illumined by the steady radiance, renewed daily, of a wonder, the source of which is beyond reason.

—Dag Hammarskjold

In a mood that is far from serene, he [Bellini] explored the same questions of beauty and ugliness, good and evil, that have always haunted the most profound interpreters of the human condition.

—David Alan Brown

It helps me when I interpret the scriptures *using* the scriptures. In other words, if the author of a particular book of scripture uses a certain phrase or expression to describe something, I look up all other uses of that expression by the same scriptural author in order to better understand what he means by it.

—Frank Hill

When men enjoy the spirit of their missions and realize their calling and standing before the Lord . . . , it constitutes the happiest portions of their lives.

—Brigham Young

My soul is not fashioned like other men's.
    To drive in their rut I might perhaps learn: To be untrue to myself could only lead to muddle.

—T'ao Ch'ien

I don't think people are comfortable in a room with too many pieces of important furniture.

—Robert Currie

A healthy outside starts from the inside.

—Robert Urich

I believe that young [people] may go through college and preserve their faith and grow in faith and intelligence and understanding if they will be faithful and true to their religious obligations, but if they do not do that, they may lose their faith.

—George Q. Morris

When anyone has offended me, I try to raise my soul so high that the offense cannot reach me.

—René Descartes

We want to see our young men qualified in every direction, so that the Lord's name may be glorified and his cause advanced through their labors and their proficiency in all the arts and sciences.

—George Q. Cannon

When do the angels come? If we seek to be worthy, they are near us when we need them most. The mountain might even be full with the horsemen of Israel and their chariots of fire.

—Bruce C. Hafen

Public TV is one of the few institutions dedicated to harnessing the awesome power of TV for public service. . . .

Today millions of American adults and children know how to read because of public TV.

—Bruce Christensen

I never saw anyone, until I met Joseph Smith, who could tell me anything about the character, personality and dwelling-place of God, or anything satisfactory about angels, or the relationship of man to his Maker.

—Brigham Young

Alma the Elder would be one of the first to remind us that praying for our young people is not a meaningless ritual or another item to check off a list. We must pray for our youth and with our youth.

—Brad Wilcox

In fact, truth *is* stranger than fiction. It's just not as *thrilling,* that's all.

—Mickey Spillane

When ideas fail, words come in very handy.

—Johann Wolfgang von Goethe

I don't think much of letters as an art form. Not even Fitzgerald, or Keats, or D. H. Lawrence, or Gertrude Bell's. They always have something ragged, domestic, undressed about them.

—T. E. Lawrence

Good criticism attempts to remedy the shortcomings of appreciation by deepening, enlarging, and objectifying our efforts.

—Robert K. Thomas

It is hard to see that one's own intimacies may be other people's common places of exchange.

—T. E. Lawrence

Well, now, when was the last time you ran to a library and took home more books than you could read, like stacked loaves of bread warm in your arms, waiting to be chewed? When, for that matter, was the last time you opened a book, placed it to your nose, and gave a great sniff? Heaven! The smell of bread baking. When was the last time that you found a really great old bookstore and wandered through it hour after hour, alone, finding yourself on the shelves? With no list, no intellectual priorities, just wandering. Sniffing the dust, plucking the pigeon books off the shelves to read their entrails and, not in love, putting them back, or, in love, toting them home? To be lost in time is to find your roots.

—Ray Bradbury

There are those speaking out against the truth and they are very apt and very determined. And *we* must be as determined to speak out and defend truth.

—Larry Bulloch

Misuse of the [English] language is widespread; so is its abuse. And both offenses are getting spread even wider day by day, particularly by television. On CBS's "Murder, She Wrote," one actress delivered to the listening millions the ungrammatical zinger: "I bought a couple of parcels for she and I."

—J. Norman McKenzie

We often repent of what we have said, but never, never, of that which we have not.

—*Thomas Jefferson*

Both heaven and hell are determined, not by the friendly or unfriendly environment, but by the individual's response to that environment. If in any experience the soul or inner man is hurt, it is due to the thoughts, actions, motives, and response of the soul itself.

—*Hugh M. Woodward*

The importance of being Alma is that his remorse over his sins was as "exquisite" as his joy after repentance. He helps us to understand the possibilities in our own choices.

—*Gordon A. Madsen*

Nature's gifts will last forever if we accept them with gratitude instead of taking them with greed.

—*David Bly*

No one buys the way we buy. No one sells the way we sell. No one cares the way we care.

—*Mac Christensen*

If we but know it, all around us are others passing through the same experiences, wrestling with the same problems, striving for the same goals.

—*William F. Kosman*

See that ye are not lifted up unto pride; . . . see that ye do not boast in your own wisdom, nor of your much strength.

Use boldness, but not overbearance; and also see that ye bridle all your passions, that ye may be filled with love; see that ye refrain from idleness.

—*Alma*

Nurture your mind with great thoughts.

—*Benjamin Disraeli*

If hunger is the permanent condition of life in the [African] camps, getting an education is the constant dream. The boys devise crude writing implements and scavenge for school supplies as they do for food. During the hardest times, groups of children often select one member to go to class while the others hunt for food. After supper they sit around a dying fire and listen avidly as their surrogate recounts the day's lesson. As the sun sets, the drone of children's voices mispronouncing English words—"bottle" becomes "boskle"—filters out of the wattle huts. In this war-torn land, the sound falls sweetly on the ear.

—*Edward Borne*

Do not dissect things too much. . . . There is a place for analysis, but it is apt to be quite fatal in prayer and meditation. . . . Pray more with your heart and less with your brain. . . . Remember the old verse:

> A centipede was happy quite,
> Until a frog in fun
> Said, "Pray, which leg comes after which?"
> This raised her mind to such a pitch,
> She lay distracted in the ditch,
> Considering how to run.

Don't be a theoretical centipede.

—Emmett Fox

Think all you speak, but speak not all you think. Thoughts are your own; your words are so no more.

—Henry Delaune

I made a resolution to keep a daily journal into which I would write any good ideas given me by others or any that I might come upon by myself. It will be eighteen years next month, and I haven't missed a day. At first this was extremely difficult, but within a year or two it became a joy.

—Leonard Read

I. O. U.

I plead with you, my brethren and my sisters, let us be generous with one another. Let us be as patient with one another as we would like others to be with us. Let us see the virtues of our neighbor and our friends, and speak of those virtues, not find fault and criticize. If we will do that we will radiate sunshine, and those who know us best will love us.

—George Albert Smith

Forgetfulness leads to exile,
While remembrance is the secret of redemption.

—Baal Shem Tov

The Bennion Center was created in 1987 to organize service opportunities and sharpen awareness within the campus community. It is named for a man [Lowell L. Bennion] whose name is synonymous with service, and it seeks to fulfill his legacy.

—Bill Dunsford

The point of manners is clarity and simplicity. A code of conduct makes it possible to understand vexing situations without starting from scratch each and every time.

—Owen Edwards

The breakthrough currently taking place is computerization of data. We have new power to search for and understand patterns in huge amounts of information.

As environmental issues become more a part of public policy, we will need this ability to better understand changes in natural communities.

—Eric Rickart

The economy may be coming back. But we're still staffed for a recession.

—Guy Millner

Historians say a sense of embattlement born in the nineteenth century still has Utah's Mormon majority acting like an oppressed minority, and wrongs committed one hundred years ago still sting today.

You can't have a people pushed across the United States in one act of persecution after another without creating a certain defensiveness.

—Mike Carter

We are part of the social change process and we are making history every day.

—Jesse Jackson

The borrower runs in his own debt.

—Ralph Waldo Emerson

The fragile veneer of civilization disintegrated in parts of Los Angeles just hours after the verdict in the Rodney King excessive force trial. On that night of April 29, self-restraint on individual behavior—once so taken for granted and the glue that holds our society together—temporarily evaporated.

—Daniel M. Kolkey

Anyone who has spent more than a week in Japan understands that its real standard of living is still far below that of Western Europe or the United States.

—James Fallows

Nothing binds us one to the other like a promise kept. Nothing divides us like a promise broken.

—Mutual Life Insurance Co.

Cities had the demographic variety, the exciting ethnic mix.
      But now, the suburbs are much more representative of the country as a whole. Many have sizable numbers of minorities. Many have institutions like symphonies and problems like poverty—once the sole province of cities.

—William Frey

LOST! Hunted by lions and hyenas, living on leaves and bark, swarms of boys wander the wilderness in a nation ravaged by a long and bloody civil war. Abandoned by adults, they are fighting a heroic battle for survival in their Republic of Children—but nobody seems to care.

A nation torn by civil war cannot care for its children—so they must care for themselves.

—*Edward Barnes*

I think that God gave us dominion over these creatures. . . . I just look at an armadillo or a skunk or a squirrel or an owl or a chicken—whatever it is—and I consider the human being on a higher scale.

—*Manuel Lujan*

Most 18-to-24-year-olds have not exercised their right to vote. Now, some citizens are sending them a message. Make your voice heard.

—*Jack Anderson*

The most important thing a nation can save is its own soul.

—*Theodore Roosevelt*

The kind of world one carries about in oneself is the important thing, and the world outside takes all its graces, color, and value from that.

—*James Russell Lowell*

Most scientists agree that all the smoke and fumes and exhaust that humans generate will eventually alter the earth's climate. Those changes could be modest. Or they could trigger coastal flooding, interior droughts, mass exoduses and pockets of starvation.

—*Phillip Elmer-Dewitt*

The men who have gone before us have taught us how to live and how to die. We are the heirs of the ages.

—*Sidney Dark*

Watergate still lives in the depths of America's troubled soul, in the nation's angry heartbeat. Watergate and Vietnam left the nation feeling betrayed. A yearning to respect the president was replaced by a haste to suspect him of the worst.

—*Donald Rothberg*

Banning smoking in state hospitals and health clinics is part of my role to protect the public and ensure good health.

—*Timothy Stamps*

We [the United States] are the cradle of the environmental movement. We spawned the new way of looking at the world. And now we are the laggard.

—*Stewart L. Udall*

The explosion [of racial tensions] in Los Angeles has redoubled calls for welfare reform, but procedural Band-Aids and fiscal tinkering won't solve the problem.

—*Thomas Saucton*

We're skeptical when politicians come visiting our communities, spending one hour on problem solving, and twelve on photo opportunities.

—*Edward F. Dempsey*

To your ailing friends give . . . chocolates which, as everyone knows, contain miracle drugs for healing. I've been sick and I know.

—*Foley Richards*

Money is never enough, it's the *manner* of the man. Make that *manners!* I want to find a way to remodel old etiquette to fit today's society.

—Owen Edwards

Today it is far worse to be accused of being anti-Semitic, anti-black, sexist, elitist, than to be known as a consummate liar or adulterer.

—E. Digby

It's the best public housing I ever saw.

—Gerald Ford

The proliferation of so many different groups—from Jamaicans to Koreans to Salvadorans—raises questions about the degree to which diverse minorities will work together.

I see a lot of competition, a lot of balkanizing of this country. There's a sense that there are scarce resources to be fought over, so it's not surprising that blacks would be very hostile toward or suspicious of new immigrants . . . or that immigrants would feel similarly toward blacks.

—Elijah Anderson

What you think of me is none of my business.

—Bryant McOmber

Yes, people have certain inalienable rights, certain freedoms, but what about decency? Doesn't society have a right to *expect* decency from each other? Innocence is precious, too, and worth holding on to. When decency in society is abandoned, innocence is lost as well.

—*James Quayle Cannon*

Have you noticed that lately every other vehicle on the freeway seems to be a little red sports car weaving in and out, going way beyond the speed limit, and it is driven by a sweet youth, certain of immortality?

—*Aldon Junior Anderson*

We all come from the past, and children ought to know what it was that went into their making, to know that life is a braided cord of humanity stretching up from time long gone, and that it cannot be defined by the span of a single journey.

—*Russell Baker*

We are in the process of creating, in sum, what deserves to be called the idiot culture. . . . Today, ordinary Americans are being stuffed with garbage. . . . The media are probably the most powerful of all our institutions today; and they are squandering their power and ignoring their obligation. They—or more precisely, we—have abdicated our responsibility, and the consequence of our abdication is the spectacle, and the triumph, of the idiot culture.

—*Carl Bernstein*

The other day I followed the humorist P. J. O'Rourke on [a talk show]. Ever provocative, he was engaging in some pretty heavy do-gooder bashing, knocking environmentalists for saying, in effect, "Because I care so much more than you do, I am morally superior to you." The implication was that we are all hypocrites, especially those of us who presume to a certain earnest humanism. In fact, there are millions of people who care more about the environment than does P. J. O'Rourke—or than I do, for that matter.

—Charles Grodin

When I was Captain of the U.S. Davis Cup team, we narrowly lost our most important match. I felt so terrible about it that I played every point of the final match over and over again in repeated sleepless nights. I started talking to myself, asking, "Why, oh why, did George Barnes [president of U.S. Lawn Tennis Association] appoint *me* Davis Cup captain?" Then one night I realized that he was probably asking himself that question. Then I figured that ten million tennis players and millions of interested spectators probably wondered the same thing. Crazy, but at last I was comforted. A warm feeling spread over me. I felt I wasn't alone! I was one with all of them. People can do that for each other.

—Dave Freed

In times of trouble, no words—no matter how magnificent—can match a helping hand.

—Frank Tyger

We need to identify what we can and cannot change [in the less-active members] and leave behind the things we can't. We should avoid telling others how the less-active feel, concentrate on their good traits, keep communication lines open with them, pray for what to do to help them, provide a bridge for the way back, maintain our own standards to provide a positive example, show due concern, support, and love for them.

—Edward J. Kimball

CHALK MARK

Be on time, know your [work], and hit the chalk mark. . . . I'm an actor—it's a job, a trade. And what you do is, too—or ought to be.

—Spencer Tracy

We must become the change we wish to see in the world.

—Mohandas K. Gandhi

Character is made by what you stand for; reputation by what you fall for.

—Alexander Woollcott

Ultimately when you change behavior, attitude change will follow. We've got some examples of that in this country. School integration. I think if we had relied upon attitudes of people to change to voluntarily integrate schools, we'd still be fighting that battle. But we passed a law which mandated behavioral change, and I think that now that kids have gone to school together and grown up together, there have been some attitude changes.

—Jay Rochlin

Learn to like what doesn't cost much.
Learn to like reading, conversation, music.
Learn to like plain food, plain service, plain cooking.
Learn to like fields, trees, brooks, hiking, rowing, climbing hills.
Learn to like people, even though some of them may be
    different . . . different from you.
Learn to like to work and enjoy the satisfaction of doing your
    job as well as it can be done.
Learn to like the songs of birds, the companionship of dogs.
Learn to like gardening, puttering around the house, and fixing
    things.
Learn to like the sunrise and sunset, the beating of rain on the
    roof and windows, and the gentle fall of snow on a winter
    day.
Learn to keep your wants simple and refuse to be controlled by
    the likes and dislikes of others.

—Lowell L. Bennion

When I make up my mind to do something, I make sure it
happens. You can't wait for the phone to ring. You have to ring
them.

—Lew Grade

Most of the change we think we see in life is due to truths
being in and out of favor.

—Robert Frost

Blood is inherited, but virtue is achieved.

—Miguel de Cervantes

I was paid a commission on the sales I made. No sales, no commission. No commission, no eat. That left a mark on me.

—Dan Ogilivy

If thou hast commenced a good action, leave it not incomplete.

—From the Talmud

How can I tell what I think till I see what I say?

—E. M. Forster

Getting out of bed in the morning is an act of false confidence.

—Jules Feiffer

Sacrifice means going without or giving up something which is good for something which is better.

—N. Eldon Tanner

The dogs bark; the caravan passes.

—Arabic proverb

Better to be good than to be original.

—*Ludwig Mies van der Rohe*

Like a lot of things in life, . . . people don't notice the poison control center until they need it.

—*Bill Dunford*

What ever happened to civility? The Eighties. It's more than knowing how to hold your knife—which *will* put you on the cutting edge of etiquette.

—*Owen Edwards*

The White House is an idea. There has never been a time when the public didn't love it.

—*William Seale*

An' ah-one, an' ah-two!

—*Lawrence Welk*

Always laugh when you can; it is a cheap medicine. Merriment is a philosophy not well understood. It is the sunny side of existence.

—*Lord Byron*

Dugway Valley lies like a discarded snake skin, ridged and dry and almost translucent in its overwhelming tanness. The antelope are out there with the falcons and coyotes on the sea of dunes and sagebrush.

—Mark Knudsen

A huge Texan, standing beside a short Alaskan, was sad because Texas was no longer the largest state.

The Alaskan, as they looked at the map, said, "Don't feel badly. We might have divided it and made *two* states bigger than Texas."

—Paul S. McElroy

The problem with scandals is that there is no way to control their repercussions once they become public property.

—Kermil Lansneto

In Mexico . . . the pervasiveness of cellular phones has quickly transformed them from status symbol to public nuisance. Some restaurants now post signs prohibiting their use at dining tables. . . . For kids there is a $5.00 toy cellular phone that's as noisy as the real thing.

—Matt Moffett

I read that the Garrick Club in London had voted 362 to 94 against admitting women to membership. As the panel moderator so often says, each of us must deal with the difficult issues in our own way.

—*Calvin Trillin*

I don't lie. I just improve on the truth.

—*Everyman*

I became mayor and, wonder of wonders, I was invited to pitch the first ball of the [baseball] season. I strode to the mound on a cool April evening. Derks [baseball field] became quiet. There is nothing quite so titillating and hushing to a crowd as the marvel of a politician about to make a fool of himself. I closed my eyes, wound up, and fired a perfect strike. The catcher said, "Suit up, man!"

—*Ted Wilson*

Other than psychiatrists, the squirrel is the only animal that lives on nuts.

—*Earl Reeves*

A man who dies too rich has lived too poorly.

—*Garff Goodbody*

Upon my weary heart were showered smiles, plaudits, and flowers; but beyond them, I saw troubles and thorns innumerable.

—*Jefferson Davis*

My advice concerning applause is this: Enjoy it, but never quite believe it.

—*Robert Montgomery*

Start every day off with a smile and get it over with.

—*W. C. Fields*

Smokers blowing smoke in my face will learn firsthand (within minutes, actually) just how injurious smoking can be to their health!

—*Herb Gossett*

POCKET CHANGE

If a book is worth reading, it is worth buying.

—John Ruskin

How do we reconcile our belief in self-government with our disbelief in politicians? Carried too far, ridicule of the people we choose to govern us may undermine self-government itself.

—Arthur M. Schlesinger, Jr.

His shoes looked as if he had shined them with a Hershey bar.

—Ned Winder

A boat is a hole in the water with wood surrounding it and money pouring in.

—T. C. Jacobsen

In the fell clutch of circumstance
I have not winced nor cried aloud.
Under the bludgeonings of chance
My head is bloody, but unbowed.

—William Ernest Henley

Methuselah ate what he found on his plate,
And never, as people do now,
Did he note the amount of the calory count;
He ate it because it was chow. . . .
He cheerfully chewed each species of food,
Unmindful of troubles or fears
Lest his health might be hurt
By some fancy dessert;
And he lived over nine hundred years.

—Author unknown

He travels the fastest who travels alone.

—Rudyard Kipling

Being disabled does not mean being unable.

—Kevin Likes

If you're going to take money out of a community, give
something back.

—Ray Kroc
(founder of McDonald's)

Strange, it wasn't until I was hospitalized that people told me
how good I looked.

—Edwin Q. Cannon, Jr.

In the councils of government, we must guard against the acquisition of unwarranted influence, whether sought or unsought, by the military-industrial complex. The potential for the disastrous rise of misplaced power exists and will persist.

—Dwight D. Eisenhower

I wonder how the organist
    Can do so many things;
He's getting ready long before
    The choir stands up and sings;
He's pressing buttons, pushing stops,
    He's pulling here and there,
And testing all the working parts
    While listening to the prayer.

—George W. Stevens

World War II was the last time in my generation when Americans of all classes pulled together.

—E. Digby Baltzell

Strange to see how a good dinner and feasting reconciles everybody.

—Samuel Pepys

Our national flower is the concrete cloverleaf.

—Lewis Mumford

The only thing to know is how to use your neuroses.

—*Arthur Adamov*

The first day of summer . . . well, it's downhill to winter now!

—*Milton L. Sharp*

In a time when it has been pronounced that we've reached the end of history, the death of rock [music] may be a very small thing.

—*Greil Marcus*

Roasting a goose seems to frighten people. It's really quite easy, if you can ignore his melancholy expression.

—*Alfred Hitchcock*

Don't point that finger; there's a nail in it.

—*Aldon J. Anderson*

Old people shouldn't eat health foods. They need all the preservatives they can get.

—*Robert Orken*

END ZONE

The tragedy of life is not that it ends so soon, but that we wait so long to begin it.

—*Richard L. Evans*

Let no man be afraid to lay down his life for my sake; for whoso layeth down his life for my sake shall find it again.

And whoso is not willing to lay down his life for my sake is not my disciple.

—*Jesus Christ*

Where do we go when we die? It all depends on where we live!

—*Milton R. Hunter*

Treasure each other in the recognition that we do not know how long we shall have each other.

—*Joshua Loth Liebman*

Be careful reading health books. You may die of a misprint.

—*Mark Twain*

At the age of sixty-seven years, his mind yet unimpaired, his iron frame unbent by age, but with health shattered by toil and trial in the service of his Maker, Heber C. Kimball, the Apostle of Jesus Christ, the tried and trusted friend of God, passed peacefully from earth away.

—Orson F. Whitney

I shall not be long after her.

—Heber C. Kimball
(following the death of his beloved wife Vilate)

Writing an autobiography and making a spiritual will are practically the same.

—Sholem Aleichem

We spend most of our time, many of us, seeking the things of this life that we will be compelled to leave when we go from here, yet there are the immortal souls around us whom, if we would, we could teach and inspire to investigate the truth and implant in their hearts a knowledge that God lives.

—George Albert Smith

What lies behind us and what lies before us are tiny matters compared to what lies within us.

—Oliver Wendell Holmes

The light of a whole life dies
   When its love is done.

—Francis W. Bourdillon

The soul of Man to God is as the flower to the sun; it opens at
its approach, and shuts when it withdraws.

—Benjamin Whichcote

Who shall ascend into the hill of the Lord? or who shall stand
in his holy place?
   He that hath clean hands, and a pure heart.

—David

Ah, but a man's reach should exceed his grasp,
   Or what's a heaven for?

—Robert Browning

I am old now and have not much to fear from the anger of the
gods. I have [no one] through whom they can hurt me. My body,
this lean carrion that still has to be washed and fed and have
clothes hung about it daily with so many changes, they may kill
as soon as they please.

—C. S. Lewis

Bury me where the birds will sing over my grave.

—*Alexander Wilson*

We are not human beings
    having a spiritual experience;
We are spiritual beings
    having a human experience.

—*Author unknown*

All the graves I walked by had dates after I was born. People were dying who were born after I was.

—*T. C. Jacobsen*

If I had known I was going to live this long I would have taken better care of myself.

—*Carl Maughn*

A great deal of talent is lost in the world for want of a little courage. Every day sends to their graves men whom timidity prevented from making a first effort; who, if they could have been induced to begin, would in all probability have gone great lengths.

—*Sidney Smith*

Being of sound mind, I videotaped my will instead of hiring a lawyer.

—Schwarsky

Oh, God, let this be heaven—
I do not ask for golden streets,
    Or long for jasper walls,
Nor do I sigh for pearly shores
    Where twilight never falls;
Just leave me here beside these peaks,
    In this rough western land,—
I love this dear old world of Thine—
    Dear God, you understand.

Oh, God, let this be heaven—
I do not crave white, stainless robes;
    I'll keep these, marked by toil;
Instead of straight and narrow walks,
    I love trails soft with soil;
I have been healed by crystal streams,
    Like these from snow-crowned peaks,
Where dawn burns incense to the day
    And paints the sky in streaks.

Dear God, let this be heaven—
I do not ask for angel wings;
    Just leave that old peak there
And let me climb till comes the night—
    I want no golden stair.
Then, when I say my last adieu
    And all farewells are given,
Just leave my spirit here somewhere—
    Oh, God, let this be heaven!

—Harrison R. Merrill

I told my comrades (who lay motionless, although occasionally a sigh could be heard) that human life, under any circumstances, never ceases to have a meaning, and that this infinite meaning of life includes suffering and dying, privation and death. . . . I said that someone looks down on each of us in difficult hours—a friend, a wife, somebody alive or dead, or a God—and he would not expect us to disappoint him.

Everything can be taken from a man but one thing; the last of the human freedoms—to choose one's attitude in any given set of circumstances, to choose one's own way.

—Viktor E. Frankl

You recollect the story of the woman who, when her only child died, in rapture looking up, as with the face of an angel, said, "I give you joy, my darling." That single sentence has gone with me years and years down through my life, quickening and comforting me.

—Henry Ward Beecher

It is not how much you know about life but how you live your life that counts. Those who can avoid mistakes by observing the mistakes of others are most apt to keep free from sorrow. In a world full of uncertainties, the record of what has gone before—human experience—is as sure and reliable as anything of which we know.

—Ray Lyman Wilbur

The moments we forgo,
Eternity itself cannot retrieve.

—*Friedrich von Schiller*

The tragedy of life is what dies inside a man while he lives.

—*Albert Schweitzer*

No, there is no escape. There is no heaven with a little hell in it—no plan to retain this or that of the devil in our hearts or our pockets. Out Satan must go, every hair and feather.

—*George Macdonald*

Men nearly all die laughing, because they know death is very terrible, and a thing to be forgotten till after it has come.

—*T. E. Lawrence*

Sweet shall be your rest if your heart does not reproach you.

—*Thomas à Kempis*

When I look upon the tombs of the great, every emotion of envy dies in me; when I read the epitaphs of the beautiful, every inordinate desire goes out; when I meet with the grief of parents upon a tombstone, my heart melts with compassion; when I see the tomb of the parents themselves, I consider the vanity of grieving for those whom we must quickly follow; when I see kings lying by those who deposed them, when I consider rival wits placed side by side, or the holy men that divided the world with their contests and disputes, I reflect with sorrow and astonishment on the little competitions, factions, and debates of mankind. When I read the several dates of the tombs, of some that died yesterday, and some six hundred years ago, I consider that great Day when we shall all of us be contemporaries, and make our appearance together.

—Joseph Addison

Death stares me in the face, waiting for its prey.

—Willard Richards

My body sleeps for a moment, but my testimony lives and shall endure forever.

—Epitaph for Orson Pratt

It is inter-woven into my character never to betray a friend or brother, my country, my religion or my God.

—Epitaph for Daniel H. Wells

There came some tests when a loved one was taken from me and my life was crushed. Part of my life was buried in the cemetery, and I wondered. Here I was struggling to help others. Why? Then I theorized that there would be no other tests that I wouldn't be able to meet. Just as I was recovering from that sorrow, a daughter died suddenly, leaving four little children motherless. That was difficult. It is still difficult to understand. But the ways of the Lord are righteous, and sometimes we have to go through experiences like these in order for us to be prepared to face the issues of today's world.

—Harold B. Lee

I have been supported under trials and troubles of every kind, yea, and in all manner of afflictions; yea, God has delivered me from prison, and from bonds, and from death; yea, and I do put my trust in him, and he will still deliver me.

—Alma

The completion of a temple means more to our minds than the mere finishing of a costly pile of masonry. It means that an enduring bond of unity between time and eternity has been welded.

—George Q. Cannon

Bear patiently, my heart, . . . for you have suffered heavier things.

—Homer

She comes gently to me and touches me on the shoulder to say,
"Come on. Buck up. Enough of this [grieving.]"

—*Pierce Brosnan*

The soul of her—the gorgeous, glowing, fervent soul of her—
surely is flaming in eager joy upon some other dawn.

—*William Allen White*

It was no uncommon thing to see boards standing at the head of
graves telling how many were scalped alive by Indians. . . . But
he, who has ever delivered his saints in all ages, protected us
from harm and danger. . . . While on this trip we milked the
cows night and morning; then after we used what milk we
needed, the rest was put in the churn, where, by the shaking of
the wagon, we had butter before noon. This we all considered a
great blessing.

—*Christopher Layton*

I went into the baptismal font and called upon Brother
McAllister to baptize me for the signers of the Declaration of
Independence, and fifty other eminent men, making one
hundred in all, including John Wesley, Columbus, and others.

—*Wilford Woodruff*

Grow old along with me!
The best is yet to be,
The last of life, for which the first was made.

—Robert Browning

Grow old along with me!
Then maybe I can stand it.

—Marve Wallin

My hand is lonely for your clasping, dear. . . . Life is short. We ought to be together, you and I.

—Henry Alford

Do not go gentle into that good night,
Old age should burn and rave at close of day;
Rage, rage against the dying of the light.

—Dylan Thomas

So the Lord blessed the latter end of Job more than his beginning.

—Job 42:12

In a free country, we are free for trash, too. But the fact that trash will always find an outlet does not mean that we should always furnish it with an outlet. And the great information conglomerates of this country are now in the trash business.

—*Carl Bernstein*

Each departed friend or loved one is a magnet that attracts us to the next world.

—*Anthony J. Cannon*

THE LAST WORD

I finish this book in the words of Robert Louis Stevenson, written as he finished one of his books:

> Go, little book, and with to all,
> Flowers in the garden, meat in the hall,
> A bin of wine, a spice of wit,
> A house with lawns enclosing it,
> A living river by the door,
> A nightingale in the sycamore!

And in the words of Southey:

> Go, little Book! from this my solitude;
> I cast thee on the waters—go thy ways:
> And if, as I believe, thy vein be good,
> The world will find thee after many days.
> Be it with thee according to thy worth:
> Go, little Book! In faith I send thee forth.

And in the words of William Wordsworth:

> Go forth, my little book! pursue thy way;
> Go forth, and please the gentle and the good.

So much for originality! Well, it is the thought that counts. Now, my own last word:

> Go forth to all them, Little Book!
> Go to the friends and associates of man.
> To the leaders of men
> And the fathers of man.
> Go to the wives, the loved ones,
> The mothers and children of men.
> Go in honor and praise, with gentle good humor
> And raise a shout in their defense.